All About Growing Orchids

Created and designed by
the editorial staff of
ORTHO BOOKS

Endorsed by the
American Orchid Society

Writer
Rick Bond

Editor
Barbara Ferguson

Major Photographer
Saxon Holt

Illustrator
Ron Hildebrand

Designer
Gary Hespenheide

Ortho Books

Editorial Director
Christine Robertson

Production Director
Ernie S. Tasaki

Managing Editors
Michael D. Smith
Sally W. Smith

System Manager
Katherine Parker

National Sales Manager
Charles H. Aydelotte

Marketing Specialist ·
Susan B. Boyle

Operations Coordinator
Georgiann Wright

Circulation Manager
Barbara F. Steadham

Administrative Assistant
Kate Rider

Senior Technical Analyst
J. A. Crozier, Jr.

Address all inquiries to
Ortho Books
Chevron Chemical Company
Consumer Products Division
Box 5047
San Ramon, CA 94583

ISBN 0-89721-151-0
Library of Congress Catalog Card
Number 87-72816

Chevron Chemical Company
6001 Bollinger Canyon Road, San Ramon, CA 94583

Acknowledgments

Consultant
Dr. Alec Pridgeon
  American Orchid Society
  West Palm Beach, Florida

Photograph Stylist
Sara Slavin

Location Scout
John Boring

Location Consultant
Diane Saeks

Copy Chief
Melinda Levine

Copyeditor
Frances Bowles

Pagination By
Linda M. Bouchard

Editorial Coordinator
Cass Dempsey

Editorial Assistant
Karen K. Johnson

Proofreader
Susan Lang

Indexer
Frances Bowles

Art Director
Craig Bergquist

Production By
Lezlly Freier

Separations By
Color Tech Corp.

Lithographed By
Webcrafters, Inc.

Photographers
Names of photographers in alphabetical order are followed by
page numbers on which their work appears. R = right,
C = center, L = left, T = top, B = bottom.
American Orchid Society: 7B, 9, 10, 29, 41CR, 41BL,
  41BR, 42R, 43TL, 43TR, 43 BL, 43BR, 67, 68L, 69, 70,
  71, 72, 73, 74R, 75, 76TL, 76R, 77, 78L, 80TL, 80BL,
  81, 83, 84, 85, 86, 87, 88, 91R, 92
Charles Marden Fitch: 20, 38TL, 38TR, 38BL, 39TL,
  39TR, 40L, 41TL, 41TR, 46, 47, 57, 68R, 74L, 76BL,
  79R, 80R, 82, 89, 90, 91L
Saxon Holt: Front cover, back cover, 4-5, 7T, 12-13, 15, 17, 18,
  19, 21, 22, 25, 26, 27, 28, 32, 37L, 37R, 44-45, 48, 52T, 52B, 53,
  54-55, 58, 60, 62-63
Pamela Peirce: 38BR, 39BL, 40R, 42L
Ortho Information Services: Title page, 24, 39BR
H. Armstrong Roberts: 59

Special Thanks To
Jeff Britt, Rod McClellan Co.
  South San Francisco, Calif.
Fordyce Orchids, Livermore, Calif.
Jim McKenna, Sausalito, Calif.
Cloellen Molinari, San Francisco, Calif.
Orchids Orinda, Livermore, Calif.
Tonkin's Orchids, Inc., Livermore, Calif.
Tim Bryden, San Francisco, Calif.
Ernie Katler, Kensington, Calif.
Craig Levitt and Steven Weaver, San Francisco, Calif.
Robert Steffi, San Francisco, Calif.
Michael Tedrick and Tom Bennett, San Francisco, Calif.
Jean and Chuck Thompson, San Francisco, Calif.

Front Cover
Miltonia, the pansy orchid, is easy to grow in cool conditions (see
page 77). This variety, *Miltoniopsis* 'Jean Carlson' is one of the
popular Colombian hybrids.

Title Page
A casual interest in orchids can easily become a consuming
hobby; a small windowsill collection can quickly expand to fill
an entire greenhouse with dazzling colors and exotic forms.

Back Cover
The size, form, and colors of *Paphiopedilum* Salty 'Val' make it
ideal for this sink-side location. This challenging hybrid is best
grown in a greenhouse, but when in flower it demands a
prominent place in the home.

ING HIDS

Orchid his ry f d with the adventures f jungle explorers, controversial theories posed by eccentric botanists, and sensational stories that rival modern-day reports of alien visitors.

5

All About Growing Orchids

ORCHIDS AS HOUSEPLANTS

Orchids have different requirements for light, humidity, water, and fertilizer than do most houseplants, but once you understand what they need, you'll find that they aren't much harder to grow.

13

SPECIAL GROWING AREAS

Special growing areas such as greenhouses and artificial-light gardens provide ideal conditions for raising orchids.

45

ORCHIDS AS A HOBBY

Orchid growing is one of the oldest and best organized of plant hobbies. Orchid societies and shows, mail-order catalogs, books, and periodicals are all available to the orchid lover.

55

ORCHID SELECTION GUIDE

This gallery of photographs and plant descriptions includes instructions for growing the orchids best suited for windowsills, light gardens, or greenhouses.

63

Introducing Orchids

Orchid history is filled with the adventures of jungle explorers, controversial theories posed by eccentric botanists, and sensational stories that rival modern-day reports of alien visitors.

Captivating in their beauty and fascinating in their complexity, orchids are easily the most colorful and intricate of all flowering plants. In the early nineteenth century when the plants were first discovered by British horticulturists, people became so taken with orchids that they reached a state popularly described as an *orchidelirium,* an ecstatic near-madness, an obsession in the truest sense of the word. At that time orchids were thought by some to have a mysteriously seductive animal essence; others simply attributed the flowers' appeal to their sublime beauty.

The fascination with orchids started in 1818 with the well-publicized blooming of a spectacular lavender cattleya, the forerunner of today's corsage orchids. The demand for these exotic and beautiful flowers was so great that orchids became big business almost overnight. Wealthy collectors and commercial nurserymen commissioned professional plant explorers to gather plants from equatorial regions around the world. Thousands of plants were collected and sent to Europe where, because of the huge demand, they were sold for very high prices.

A collection of prize-winning paphiopedilum hybrids will steal the show in any room. From left to right are Paphiopedilum *Neptune 'Mars', Delrosi, Winston Churchill 'Indomitable', Maudiae 'Los Osos', and Kay Rinaman 'Val'.*

The plant explorers endured many hardships—dangerous voyages, cannibalistic natives, thieves, and exotic diseases—but the orchids and the trees that bore them suffered far worse. To get their prizes, the hunters chopped down entire trees, stripped the orchids from the fallen branches, and packed the plants into crates. The crates were then hauled to the nearest port where they often sat for days or even weeks before being stuffed into the dark, dank holds of ships. Once aboard, the orchids had to endure long voyages on the high seas to England, France, or the United States.

Not surprisingly, few of the plants survived the trip. Those that lived long enough to reach the greenhouses of collectors were subjected to the most trying of growing conditions. Before the mid-1800s most orchid growers shared the misconception that their plants had been gathered from dark, steamy jungles. When the plants arrived growers put the orchids in "stove houses," sooty, steamy greenhouses heated to unbearable temperatures by coal- or wood-burning stoves. They thought that this duplicated the natural conditions. No ventilation was provided for fear the steam and heat would escape. To us this kind of treatment hardly seems favorable to any kind of life, but at that time people rarely ventilated their own living spaces, believing that drafts of air led to a number of fatal diseases. Against such odds, even the toughest orchids from the cool, breezy mountains of the tropics hardly had a chance.

As proof of their enduring nature, enough orchids did survive and bloom to fuel the Victorian demand for more plants. For over a hundred years, wealthy orchid hobbyists and their suppliers spent fortunes sponsoring explorers in search of new species—species they could name after themselves, their friends, and their families. The not-so-privileged public was also fascinated by orchids, and crowds flocked to orchid shows, lured by the imaginative stories of writers such as H.G. Wells who portrayed orchids as sinister plants with a thirst for human blood.

This mania wasn't just a Victorian fad. The mystique of orchid growing, combined with the endless possibilities of hybridization, continues to enthrall hobbyists around the world. Today professional orchid growers will pay up

The Interior of a Stove House

to $25,000 for a single new hybrid. Orchid societies meet regularly throughout the world to trade plants and tips, and their dazzling shows of artfully composed miniature landscapes filled with stunning hybrids outshine the wildest dreams of the Victorians.

Why all the fuss over orchids? They are obviously very beautiful, but so are many other flowers. What makes orchids so special? Part of it is a mystery, simply an unexplainable emotional reaction, but part is based in science. As botanists will explain, orchid flowers are the most advanced and intricate in the entire plant kingdom. In their evolution, orchids have become specialized, developing complex mechanisms that cause insects and other animals to pollinate their blossoms. The result is an amazing variety of fanciful, sometimes bizarre, flower forms and colors.

BOTANICAL SOPHISTICATION: FLOWERS AND POLLINATORS

Charles Darwin was one of the first to study the remarkable ways in which orchids attract insects. He observed that the nectar produced by the flowers of *Angraecum sesquipedale* (a species from the island of Madagascar) was held at the very bottom of a long, pointed tube, far out of the reach of any insect he had ever seen. Assuming that this nectar attracted pollinators as it does in other flowers, he postulated that angraecum flowers must be pollinated by a "huge moth, with a wonderfully long proboscis" capable of tapping the nectar. Forty years later Darwin's hypothesis proved correct when scientists on Madagascar found the very moths he had envisaged.

This was just the beginning. As more orchids were studied, botanists were astounded by the variety and sophistication of their colors and structures. They were particularly amazed by the way some orchids mimic the appearance and odors of female insects in order to inspire the amorous attentions of males—a phenomenon the scientists delicately dubbed "pseudocopulation." Orchids in the genus *Ophrys* seem to have perfected this seductive mimicry, enhancing their uncanny resemblance to female wasps or flies with a fragrance nearly identical to the insects' sex attractant. But when a male attempts to mate with one of these flowers, all it gets for its trouble are pollinia (clumps of pollen) to transfer to another flower where the insect is duped again.

Victorian scientists were reluctant to publish their embarrassing discoveries and earnestly proposed alternative explanations. One botanist even asserted that the resemblance of a particular *Ophrys* species to a fly had nothing to do with pollination; he said it served to frighten away browsing cows.

Left: By simply observing this flower, Angraecum sesquipedale, *Charles Darwin was able to predict the size of the moth that pollinated it.*
Above: When an orchid flower is pollinated, it quickly fades and the plant sets about the business of making seeds— thousands of them. This immature pod has been opened to reveal clumps of seeds. An orchid seed is one of the smallest in the plant kingdom, as minute as a speck of dust.

Other Tricks

Not all orchid mimicry is seductive. Some *Oncidium* species challenge the territorial instincts of bees by dangling their threatening (to the bees, anyway) flowers at the ends of long, slender stalks, a trick botanists call "pseudoantagonism." When the flowers move in the breeze, the bees attack. After furiously bumping the flowers like airborne bulls, the bees come away with wads of pollen stuck to their foreheads, pollen they can't help but transfer to other flowers in ensuing battles.

Some paphiopedilums pander to the appetites of flies with the foul (but luckily faint) fragrance of rotting fruit or meat. Lurid brown, green, and purple petals with fuzzy black warts resembling clusters of flies complete the effect. When a fly lands on the flower thinking it is joining other flies for a meal, it can't hold on to the slippery surface and slides off into a large pouch formed by the flower's lower petal. The fly can only escape by crawling up a narrow tunnel, rubbing off any pollen it received from other flowers and picking up a new load just before it leaves.

Coryanthes speciosa, the bucket orchid, has one of the most impressive trapping mechanisms of all. In the early morning, it produces a delightful fragrance that attracts bees. The part of the flower that produces this fragrance is very slippery and is positioned just above glands that secrete fluid into the bucket. Because the flower is so slippery, the bee slides into the bucket, thoroughly wetting its wings and preventing flight. After some frantic struggling, the bee finds a way out through a narrow tunnel at one end of the bucket. It clambers up through this tunnel and emerges with pollinia stuck to its body. The next day the bee, recovered from its ordeal but still carrying its payload of pollen, becomes overwhelmed by the fragrance of another bucket orchid. This time some of the pollen rubs off while the bee is escaping through the tunnel and the flower becomes cross-pollinated.

FLOWER STRUCTURES

Orchids accomplish their reproductive feats with fanciful variations on a theme of three petals and three sepals. In cattleyas, these parts are easily identified. The two uppermost petals are brightly colored; the highly modi-

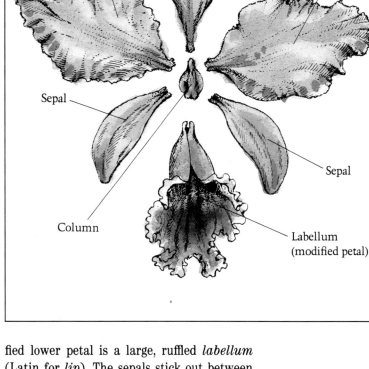

Parts of a Typical Orchid Blossom

Petal

Sepal

Petal

Sepal

Sepal

Column

Labellum (modified petal)

fied lower petal is a large, ruffled *labellum* (Latin for *lip*). The sepals stick out between and behind the petals like the points of a three-pointed star.

The labellum is often the largest and most colorful part of an orchid flower. It can take many different forms. In the slipper orchids, the labellum forms a slipper-shaped pouch. In many oncidium flowers, it fans out like a skirt, inspiring the name "dancing dolls."

Orchids share this combination of three petals and three sepals with lilies, causing some lilies to be mistaken for orchids. Orchids, however, are distinguished from other flowers by the column, an intricate structure formed by the fused male and female reproductive parts—the stamen and pistil. Although the stamen and pistil are very close together on the column, self-pollination is prevented by a divider called the rostellum. Self-pollination may also be prevented by a variety of other mechanisms, most of which are designed to attach pollen to an insect after it has passed the pistil and is on its way out of the flower.

The column can be the most interesting part of an orchid flower. Some columns look like the faces of humans, insects, or birds; others look like African masks. They may bear wings or wear caps, goggles, or bonnets.

Pollination: Traps and Triggers

Given their elaborate tricks for attracting insects, it is not surprising that orchids have equally effective methods for ensuring that their visitors are well-supplied with pollen when they leave. Orchid pollen, usually massed into the clumps called pollinia, is different from the fluffy powder produced by most other insect-pollinated plants.

In cattleyas, an insect (usually a bee) is lured under the column by a supply of nectar or by the flower's enticing fragrance. On its way out, the bee's back becomes coated with a sticky adhesive that catches and attaches one or more of the pollinia.

The pollinia in a catasetum orchid are spring-loaded. When a bee bumps the trigger, the pollinia are ejected from the flower onto the insect's body, where they stick tightly. If you trigger the flower with the tip of a pencil held out of the line of fire, the pollinia can shoot several feet.

Abundant Flowers

Orchid flowers are borne in clusters on stalks. A stalk of flowers (known to botanists as an inflorescence) is commonly called a spike. From a botanical standpoint, however, the word *spike* is used to describe flowers that are attached directly to the flower stalk, an arrangement infrequently found in the orchid family. Orchid flowers are usually attached to the main stalk (the peduncle) by a smaller stalk (the pedicel). Depending on the branching pattern and maturation of the flowers, an inflorescence may be called a raceme, panicle, corymb, or cyme. In this book we will simply use the word *spike* as it is most commonly used—to refer to a stalk of flowers.

Most orchids bear more than one flower on a spike. Some brassias, for example, may have hundreds of flowers on a spike several feet long. The flowers at the base will often open before those at the tip, but because the flowers last a long time, many plants will dazzle you by displaying nearly all of their flowers for most of the time the plant is in bloom.

FLORAL LONGEVITY

Orchid flowers look durable, and they are. Waxy paphiopedilum blossoms last for over a month. Phalaenopsis flowers can linger for up to three months. Also, the spikes of phalaenopsis, oncidium, and other orchids often send out side branches with new flower buds after the main flowers on the spike have faded. In this way, a plant may remain in bloom for six to eight months.

Obviously orchids don't display their flowers for such long periods simply for the delight of their admirers. They are holding out for insects to come along and pollinate them. Once fertilized, orchid flowers quickly fade and the plant turns to the business of making seed. Unless a member of the appropriate species of fly or bee happens into your home, or you pollinate the flowers yourself, your plants will remain in bloom until the flowers die.

ORCHID HABITATS

Orchids are found all over the world, in all but the harshest climates of permanent frost or unrelieved aridity. Over 25,000 species have been named so far, and new ones are discovered every year. About 150 of these species are native to North America. Europe is home to a similar number of species. Although another 500 orchids hail from Australia, by far the majority live in the tropical regions of Central and South America, Africa, Madagascar, Asia, and New Guinea.

Compared with the tropical areas of the world, North America is home to relatively few orchid species. The North American cypripediums, however, are prized by orchid fanciers around the world. This well-grown specimen is Cypripedium calceolus var. parviflorum *'Carrie Ann'.*

Epiphytes and Terrestrials

In the tropics, some orchids live in the humus-rich soil at the edges of streams, in clearings, and other spots on the ground where the dense shade is dappled by patches of sunlight. These orchids are terrestrial, that is, they live on the ground. In most parts of a tropical forest, however, there simply isn't enough sunlight at ground level to support many flowering plants. Thus, most tropical orchids are epiphytes (tree-dwellers) that have adapted to living up above the ground where the light is more plentiful. When Darwin first saw epiphytic orchids clinging to the branches of their hosts, he thought they were parasites, drawing their nourishment from their hosts through tenacious, leechlike roots.

Actually, orchids use the branches of trees only as a place to live. They absorb their nutrients, not from their hosts, but from the decaying organic matter that accumulates around their roots and photosynthesize sugars from the sunlight streaming through the gaps in the leafy canopy. They damage trees only when they grow too heavy for the branches to bear; occasionally massive colonies of orchids crash to the forest floor.

In adapting to their aerial environment, epiphytic orchids developed thick roots, coated with a spongy material that allows them to stick to the bark of trees and absorb water rapidly. To survive periods of drought, many species have pseudobulbs, thickened stems that can store both water and food. In other epiphytic species, the leaves themselves are thickened storage organs.

Most of the terrestrial orchids we grow, such as paphiopedilums, aren't all that different from their tree-dwelling relatives. Because they generally live in rich, fluffy humus, their roots resemble those of the epiphytes and have similar needs for water, air, and fertilizer. To further blur the distinction, some epiphytes end up living as terrestrials when they fall out of a tree into a sunny spot.

Two terrestrials that could never be mistaken for epiphytes are the Australian orchids *Rhizanthella gardneri* and *Cryptanthemis slateri*. These bizarre species grow underground, seeing the light of day only when flowering and dispersing seed. Scientists know very little about these oddities; their subterranean habits make them rather hard to study.

PATTERNS OF GROWTH

Orchids have two basic growth patterns: monopodial and sympodial. A monopodial orchid grows predominantly upward. It has a main stem, which produces new leaves at the tip and flowers from buds at the juncture of the leaves and stem. The word *monopodial* (Latin for *single foot*) describes this type of single-stem growth habit. Vandas and phalaenopsis are common monopodial orchids.

A sympodial orchid grows outward along the surface of the growing medium; its stem

Left: Orchids and bromeliads adorn the branches of trees throughout the tropics. Dead trees seem to come back to life when covered by a colony of orchids. Even a fence post can host an orchid or two. Opposite above: Phalaenopsis, the moth orchid, has a monopodial growth habit. Opposite below: Oncidium, the dancing doll orchid, is sympodial.

Monopodial Growth Habit

Sympodial Growth Habit

(called a rhizome) is often horizontal. New shoots originate from buds on the rhizome and send out their own roots. The flower spikes of sympodial orchids may originate from the base of the plant or from between the leaves at the top. *Sympodial* (Latin for *many footed*) describes their spreading growth habit. Cattleyas and paphiopedilums are familiar examples of sympodial orchids.

Orchid biology is fascinating. An awareness of the ways in which orchids are designed—how they absorb moisture and nutrients, grow with a tenacious grip on other plants and rocks, and produce such intricately structured flowers—will enhance your enjoyment of them. If you are interested in learning more about orchid biology, many books and periodicals cover this subject more thoroughly (see Sources, page 61).

If you aren't captivated by the nuances of orchid anatomy, all you really need to know in order to grow these plants is how to provide them with the proper amounts of light, air, water, and fertilizer. Orchids aren't necessarily harder to grow than other houseplants; they are just different. In the following chapter, "Orchids as Houseplants," you'll learn what these differences are and find out how to create an orchid garden in your home.

Orchids as Houseplants

Most orchids grow on trees and, therefore, have different requirements for light, humidity, water, and fertilizer than do plants that grow in soil. Once you understand the conditions that orchids need, you'll find that they aren't much harder to grow than other houseplants.

Orchids have a reputation for being difficult, finicky plants that require the heat and humidity of a tropical jungle—not the kind of climate you would like to create in your living room. Although some orchids are found in steamy jungles, most others grow in far more pleasant climates. In fact, the orchid family is one of the most widely adapted of all plant families. Orchids of one species or another grow all over the world, except in the most severe arctic and desert areas. This adaptive diversity offers you the opportunity to choose plants that can be grown with a minimum of effort in your home. All you need to do is define the conditions you have or can easily provide and then select the plants that you like and that will adapt to your environment.

The first step in creating a growing area for orchids is to take a close look at the available conditions. How much light is there? What is the temperature range? These factors are the ones you will most likely want to accept at first, because they are the most difficult and expensive to modify. But other important factors, such as humidity and ventilation, can easily be altered. The amount of light, heat, water, and air that orchids require is described in the following section. Use this information to help determine the type of orchid environment you can most easily provide.

Adapting easily to the indirect light of a bright room, a group of phalaenopsis orchids makes a stunning and long-lasting centerpiece.

LIGHT

Like most other flowering plants, orchids often grow and bloom best in as much light as they can tolerate without burning. Thus, if there are several spots in your home where you might want to grow orchids, the brightest is nearly always the best. An unobstructed south-facing window is ideal because it receives bright light for most of the day and will usually capture enough light to carry the plants through the winter months. However, you need to be careful in the summer; a south-facing window can burn even the most light-demanding species. A number of orchids will also thrive in east- or west-facing windows, but keep in mind that the duration of light is as important as the brightness—two hours of searing afternoon sunlight are no substitute for six hours of diffuse radiance. Plants can use only so much light energy; any extra just heats up the leaves.

The direction a window faces gives only a general indication of how much light is available to the plants inside. Many windows are partially shaded by outdoor plants or roof overhangs, and outdoor light levels vary from region to region. Also, the color and texture of the walls and other surfaces inside the window will influence the intensity of light in the room. For these reasons, many growers shy away from imprecise descriptions of exposure and discuss light in terms of a standard measurement, the footcandle.

Measuring Light

A footcandle is the amount of light falling on a 1-square-foot surface located 1 foot away from one candle. Unless you do your evening reading as Abraham Lincoln did, this probably doesn't mean much to you. Here are some more familiar examples: The light intensity outdoors at noon on a clear summer day may be as high as 10,000 footcandles; a midday reading on an overcast winter day may be as low as 500 footcandles. As you would expect, the intensity of light indoors is much lower. The direct sunlight entering a window on a clear summer day may be as high as 8,000 footcandles next to the glass, but is usually closer to 4,000 to 5,000 footcandles. At the same time, the intensity of light in the shade to the side of a very bright window may only be 600 footcandles. The brightness of artificial lights can be deceiving. A supermarket seems very bright, but the light intensity is usually only about 500 footcandles.

Because our pupils adjust so effectively to light, we can't really estimate light intensity just by looking. The easiest and most accurate way to learn how much light is available to the plants is to measure it with a footcandle light meter (see Sources, page 61). Be sure to purchase a meter that can measure light intensities at least as high as 5,000 footcandles. The most commonly used meter, made by General Electric, has a filter that clips over the sensor for use at high light intensities.

If you don't want to purchase a light meter that measures light in footcandles, you can estimate light intensity using a photographic meter or a camera with a built-in light meter. Most cameras have meters that measure light intensity in f-stops. See Using a Camera to Measure Light (below), for instructions on converting f-stops to footcandles.

Using a Camera to Measure Light

Any camera with a built-in light meter will provide fairly accurate readings that can be translated into footcandles. Set the film speed at ASA 25 and the shutter speed at 1/60 second. Aim the camera at a flat sheet of matte white paper or cardboard, held at the level where the plant's leaves would be. Hold the camera close enough so that all you see when you look through the viewfinder is the paper. Be sure not to block the light with your head, hands, or camera. Adjust the f-stop (lens opening) until a correct exposure for taking a picture is shown on the light meter in the camera. Use the table below to convert the f-stop setting into a footcandle estimate.

f-stop	Footcandles
f/2.8	200
f/4	370
f/5.6	750
f/8	1,500
f/11	2,800
f/16	5,000

For best results, take the readings at the brightest time of a sunny day, preferably in summer. This will give you an idea of the maximum intensity to which the plants will be exposed and will enable you to avoid scorching them with too much light. The average light intensity (of long-term importance to growth and flowering) is harder to measure accurately, but you can estimate it by taking readings at different times over a period of several days.

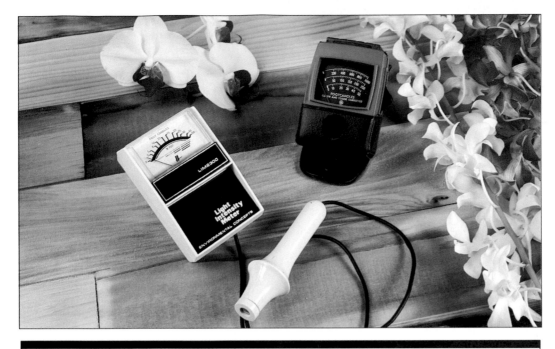

The most accurate way to make sure that plants are receiving enough light is to measure the light intensity with a footcandle light meter. The meter on the left has a separate sensor to allow you to easily read the dial while measuring the light from different angles. The meter on the right has a sensor built into the top of the unit.

Ideal Light Ranges

	Low		Medium		High	
500	1,000	1,500	2,000	2,500	3,000	3,500	4,000

Brassavola

Brassia

Cattleya

Cymbidium
 standard
 miniature

Dendrobium

Epidendrum

Laelia

Ludisia

Masdevallia

Miltonia

Odontoglossum

Oncidium

Paphiopedilum
 green-leaf
 mottled-leaf

Phalaenopsis

Phragmipedium

Sophronitis

Vanda

Light Requirements

Once you've measured the light intensity in your growing area, you can begin to choose the kinds of orchids that will grow best for you. The chart on page 15 shows the light requirements of the orchids described in this book. Notice that most of these orchids will adapt to light intensities in the medium range—1,500 to 3,000 footcandles. Some species within a genus—or some of their innumerable hybrids—may be exceptions. An intergeneric hybrid (created by crossing plants in two different genera) may tolerate a broader range of light intensities than can either parent. Before purchasing a new plant, find out about its light requirements.

If you have some orchids, the most practical way to see if they are receiving the right amount of light is to look at the plants themselves. When orchids are receiving enough but not too much light, the leaves are light- to medium-green and the pseudobulbs are full and firm. The plants also bloom dependably if other conditions are right.

With too little light, the leaves are unable to manufacture enough food for the plant to grow and bloom well. Growth is elongated, flimsy, and dark green. Pseudobulbs are soft and sometimes shriveled. And the flowers—if they appear at all—are faded and floppy.

At the other extreme, orchids that get too much light are often very obviously scorched.

Short of scorching, the leaves may have a yellow or reddish tinge. And, although the plant may bloom, the flower buds and racemes may be deformed, a result of water stress.

Direct sunlight can burn orchids during the brightest hours from late winter to fall in most regions, or even year-round in southern latitudes and at high elevations. Generally, plants with thick leathery leaves are slow to burn, and plants with thin leaves burn easily.

Modifying Light

Diffusing midday sunlight, making some shade, or otherwise reducing the intensity of sunlight on your orchids poses no problem. Easily opened sheer or open-weave curtains may be all you need. Blinds are ideal because they can be adjusted to allow just the right amount of light to fall on the plants. The moving bars of sunlight shining through the slats of a blind mimic the play of dappled light through the leaves of trees.

You may not need to cover the windows with anything if you can move the plants back a few feet; light intensity decreases rapidly as you move away from the source.

If the light coming in through the windows is too dim to sustain the kinds of orchids you want to grow, don't give up hope; many orchids thrive under artificial lights. See the chapter "Special Growing Areas" (page 45) for information about light gardens.

Light Tips

Light is a key ingredient in successful orchid growing. Too much light will burn the leaves, too little light—or light at the wrong time—will keep the plants from flowering. Follow these tips to make sure your plants are getting the illumination they need.

☐ Turn plants occasionally to keep them from becoming lopsided. Don't turn them when they are in bud, though, or the flowers may twist around at awkward angles to face the sun.

☐ Move an underexposed orchid into stronger light one step at a time over a period of several weeks. If you are using a light meter, try to increase the light intensity by no more than 100 to 200 footcandles at a time.

☐ Remove plants from full sun once their flowers have opened. Bright sunlight can make the colors fade.

☐ Watch new acquisitions closely to be sure they don't burn before they adapt to stronger exposures than that to which they are accustomed.

☐ If you suspect a plant is receiving too much sun, feel the leaves. If they are much warmer than the surrounding air, reduce the light intensity.

☐ Keep your plants and windows clean—dust and dirt block sunlight.

☐ Some orchids need a period of uninterrupted darkness at night in order to flower. Plants growing in a living area may be prevented from flowering by the illumination of a single table lamp. If a certain type of orchid is light sensitive, this is noted in the "Orchid Selection Guide" (page 63).

TEMPERATURE

In nature, the temperature begins to drop when the sun sets and is at its lowest just before dawn. Orchids are accustomed to this temperature fluctuation and, in fact, most of them depend on it. Without a day-night fluctuation of 10° to 15° F, the plants will grow plenty of healthy foliage, but may stubbornly refuse to flower. Cool nighttime temperatures allow them to store rather than expend the carbohydrates they manufacture during the day—the carbohydrates they need to produce those beautiful blossoms.

To make it easier to describe the temperature needs of orchids, orchid growers divide the plants into three temperature categories: warm, intermediate, and cool. Although the exact temperatures associated with these terms varies (some growers use wider ranges), the following ranges are most common:

	Day (° F)	Night (° F)
Warm	75–85	65–70
Intermediate	65–75	55–65
Cool	60–70	50–55

Most orchids, like most people, prefer temperatures in the intermediate range. Given adequate humidity and ventilation, many orchids will tolerate higher daytime temperatures than those shown above—as long as they cool off at night. Thus, the night temperature is the most important temperature factor to consider when selecting orchids. Although some determined hobbyists have used space heaters, infrared lights, and heating cables to create a warm spot in their homes for orchids, such efforts are only necessary if you are trying to grow plants that require much warmer temperatures than those you can naturally provide. It is much more practical to find out what temperatures you have and select the plants accordingly.

Measuring Temperature

Unless you spend a great deal of time at home during the day and get up before dawn each morning, you may find you don't really know the maximum and minimum temperatures in your orchid-growing area. A special kind of thermometer, appropriately called a maximum-minimum thermometer, can measure these temperatures for you. A maximum-minimum thermometer generally has two sides;

one side records the high temperature and the other records the low. It also displays the current temperature. Mount the thermometer as close to the plants as possible, but keep it out of direct sunlight. Many orchid supply companies offer maximum-minimum thermometers; see Sources on page 61 for their addresses.

Temperature Requirements

The chart on page 18 shows the ideal night temperature ranges for the kinds of orchids in this book. You will notice that many kinds will grow in more than one temperature category. This may be a reflection of the orchid's adaptability or it may be a result of plant breeding; many hybrids are much more adaptable than their parents. For example, a hybrid produced by crossing a cool-growing parent with an intermediate-growing parent may grow well in either temperature range.

Tiny needles in the glass tubes of a maximum-minimum thermometer are pushed by the mercury as the temperature changes. To determine the maximum and the minimum temperatures, read the bottoms of the needles against the scale. In this case, the minimum temperature is 62° F. The maximum temperature is 81° F. You reset the thermometer by pulling the needles back to the mercury with a small magnet.

Ideal Night Temperature Ranges

	Cool		Intermediate		Warm
	50	55	60	65	70
Brassavola					
Brassia					
Cattleya					
Cymbidium					
standard					
miniature					
Dendrobium					
Epidendrum					
Laelia					
Ludisia					
Masdevallia					
Miltonia					
Odontoglossum					
Oncidium					
Paphiopedilum					
green-leaf					
mottled-leaf					
Phalaenopsis					
Phragmipedium					
Sophronitis					
Vanda					

Left: Often all you have to do to adjust the temperature is open a window. The orchids on this window shelf are bathed by a cool San Francisco breeze. A few succulents thrive in the bright light enjoyed by the orchids.
Opposite: The large dial of this hygrometer makes it possible to tell at a glance if the air contains enough moisture for orchids.

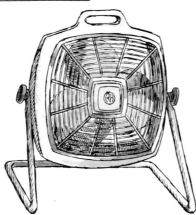

Temperature Tips

The temperature can vary quite a bit within a growing area. At night, it is coolest next to the windows and near the floor. During the day, the air next to the glass becomes the warmest air in the room. You can take advantage of these small-scale variations in temperature or eliminate them by mixing the air with a fan.

☐ Place orchids with lower temperature needs closer to the floor and those with higher temperature needs on shelves above them.

☐ Hang plastic curtains around windows to create microclimates that are cooler at night and warmer during the day.

☐ Don't let plants touch the windows in the winter in cold regions.

☐ Use a fan to circulate warm air or bring cool air in from another part of the house.

Modifying Temperature

Many people customarily turn their thermostats down at night to 55° to 60° F to conserve energy. In addition to reducing the heating bill, this practice also satisfies the cool-night requirements of orchids. In a well-insulated house, however, the temperature may not drop low enough. If this is the case, consider opening a window to allow the evening breezes to cool the plants. Ideally, an "orchid room" can be separated at night from the rest of the house by a closed door. The temperature in that room can then be allowed to drop without chilling the rest of the home.

HUMIDITY

Most orchids grow best in a relative daytime humidity of about 40 to 70 percent. Humidity is moisture in the air, not water on the plants or in the growing medium. Airborne moisture keeps the plants from drying out in bright light and warm air, without encouraging the fungi and bacteria that can infect wet plants.

Measuring Humidity

An experienced orchid grower can tell whether the humidity is right by sniffing the air—or so some claim. Hygrometers (instruments that measure humidity) are much more reliable. The simplest and least expensive hygrometers have a dial that shows the percentage of relative humidity. A fibrous material (the old ones used a hair) connected to the needle shrinks and swells depending on the humidity. More accurate (and more expensive) hygrometers are a combination of two thermometers. One of the thermometers measures the wet bulb temperature, the temperature of evaporating water; the other measures the dry bulb, or air temperature. By consulting a table you can convert these temperatures to relative humidity. For most hobbyists, the inexpensive dial-type hygrometer is sufficient. Many orchid supply companies carry hygrometers. See Sources on page 61 for their addresses.

Raising Humidity

Relative humidity falls as the temperature rises. To keep plants from drying out, you want to reverse this process. The simplest way to raise the humidity around plants is to grow them on trays or saucers filled with water and

A water-filled tray of gravel adds moisture to the air and keeps the growing mediums in the pots from drying out too quickly.

Humidity Tips

There are many ways to increase the humidity in a growing area. Here are some pointers for care of evaporation trays and some ideas for maintaining the moisture in the air around your plants.

☐ Remove the pebbles from your evaporation tray every two or three months and wash them in a weak bleach solution to remove accumulated salts and algae. Do *not* add bleach or algaecide to water in the trays when they are in use.

☐ Use a turkey baster to remove excess water from the trays after you water your plants.

☐ Mist your plants only if they will have plenty of time to dry off before nightfall.

☐ Plants themselves are effective humidifiers. Group your plants to create an attractive display and humid microclimate, but don't place them so close that they restrict air circulation.

☐ Adjust the vents of your heating system so that the warm, dry air does not blow directly onto the plants.

☐ Drape plastic sheets around growing areas such as flower carts or windowsills to retain the moisture released by the gravel trays and plants. Allow some ventilation.

gravel. Choose trays that are 100-percent watertight; plastic and fiberglass are the most reliable. The tray should be a minimum of 1½ inches deep, filled to the rim with ¼- to 1-inch gravel. Keep the water level in the tray within 1 inch of the surface. This allows the gravel to remain moist but keeps the water from saturating the bottoms of the pots. The air circulating through this layer of moist gravel provides humidity for the plants.

Raising the humidity by using gravel trays is not always effective—especially if the air is extremely dry or if there is a lot of air movement around the plants. The bit of moist air from the trays dries up or is circulated away too quickly to be of much help. If gravel trays are not doing the job, drape a plastic sheet around the collection, but don't make it too airtight. Some air circulation is required.

You may want to enhance the humidifying action of the tray by placing a heating cable in the gravel. These cables, commonly sold in garden centers for seed germination flats, come in various lengths and have built-in thermostats that turn them on if the temperature drops below 74° F. Arrange the cable in S-shaped loops on the bottom of an empty tray so the loops are 3 to 4 inches apart. Then slowly add the gravel, making sure that the cables do not touch. Although cables do not heat the air around the plants to any significant extent, they may provide a margin of protection on cold nights.

Many types of trays are offered by indoor gardening suppliers (see Sources, page 61). "Egg carton" trays are used without gravel, which makes them easier to clean and carry. A waffle pattern inside the tray holds the pots above the water. You can also place a sheet of ½-inch plastic lighting diffuser grate in the bottom of a tray to create your own egg carton tray. Diffuser grates are available at most do-it-yourself stores.

Plants are also effective humidifiers. By arranging your orchids in groups with ferns and other moisture-loving plants, you can raise the humidity and, at the same time, create a very attractive display.

Room humidifiers are very popular because humidity is thought to be beneficial to people. These humidifiers also provide a fine atmosphere for orchids. The old steam vaporizers commonly used in sickrooms have largely been replaced by cool-mist humidifiers. The least expensive cool-mist humidifiers have a motor and fan assembly that breaks the water into fine droplets and propels them out a vent in the top. More expensive models use high-frequency sound waves (higher than we can hear) to create a fine, cool mist. These "ultrasonic" humidifiers usually have water filters that remove the minerals that would otherwise settle out as fine white dust on your plants and furniture. Some have programmable timers; others have a built-in hygrometer that automatically turns them on when the humidity drops below a certain level. Ultrasonic humidifiers are more expensive (ranging from $75 to $100), but most people prefer their automatic features and silent operation.

Misting, although commonly recommended and practiced, probably provides more enjoyment for the grower than humidity for the plants. If your plants are in an eastern window, a morning spritzing might raise the humidity enough to carry them through the bright morning hours. But, in most cases, misting only provides five minutes of relief for a 24-hour problem. You won't harm the plants by misting them unless you spray them too

frequently or late in the afternoon when their wet leaves may invite infection by pathogens. Just don't try to solve a humidity problem with a mist bottle. If your house is impossibly dry and you don't want to invest in a humidifier, consider growing orchids in an orchid case. These cases are described in the chapter on "Special Growing Areas," beginning on page 45.

AIR MOVEMENT

Gentle air movement helps your orchids in many ways. Moving air cools the leaves, allowing the plants to tolerate high light intensities without burning. It also evaporates water on the surfaces of the leaves and in the cracks between them, reducing the risk of infection by fungi and bacteria. A gentle breeze eliminates pockets of cold air that may form next to the windows or along the floor.

The air movement produced by a ceiling fan mimics the gentle breezes in the leafy canopy of a tropical cloud forest.

The need for ventilation is often emphasized in orchid books written for energy-conscious greenhouse growers, but it is less of a problem for home hobbyists. Still, if your home is very well sealed, indoor pollutants from pilot lights, cooking, smoking, and aerosol sprays can build up to levels that will damage orchid flowers.

Obviously, the easiest way to ventilate a windowsill garden is to open the windows. Don't open them too wide, though—strong drafts can rapidly dry the plants and a gust of wind can knock them over. Double-hung windows work well because they can be opened from the top, allowing air to circulate through the room without creating drafts or gales.

If it is too hot or too cold to open the windows, circulate the air with a small fan, directed away from the plants. Ceiling fans are quiet, inexpensive to run, and delightful.

WATER

Overwatering is the major cause of death or damage to orchid plants. Most beginning orchid growers, assuming that tropical plants need to be kept continuously wet, overwater their plants. Although it is true that the forest habitats of many of our most treasured orchids are very moist, the plants themselves grow in some of the driest spots in these forests—in the trees. Because there is no soil to hold moisture for them between rainstorms, epiphytic (tree-growing) orchids have evolved special roots that enable them to capture and retain the water that briefly falls on them. These roots are sheathed with a white, spongy material called velamen. Velamen absorbs moisture from rain or dew and holds it until it is drawn into the pseudobulbs and leaves.

But roots don't just need water—they also need air. When the velamen on a root remains saturated for too long, the inside of the root suffocates and begins to rot. Thus, although velamen performs a very positive function for a plant on a tree, it can be a liability for a plant in an overwatered container.

Some beginning orchid growers are alarmed to find their plants sending roots straight out into the open air. This is natural. They may look a bit unruly at first, but you'll probably soon agree that these roots add to the plants' charm. They should not be cut off, forced into the medium, or otherwise disturbed.

When to Water

How can you tell when to water? There are many variables: Some types of orchids require more water than others, and some have rest periods when they should receive little or no water. These specifics are described for each type of plant in the "Orchid Selection Guide" beginning on page 63. Also, the type of pot and growing medium the plant is in will influence its need for water, as will the light intensity and other environmental factors discussed earlier. Despite these factors and exceptions, it is still possible to offer a few general (and generally safe) guidelines.

Epiphytic orchids with pseudobulbs or orchids with very succulent leaves should be watered when the potting medium is almost completely dry. To test for dryness, press your finger into the medium. If it feels moist, wait a day or two and test it again before watering it. If it is dry to the touch, the plant should be watered.

If you prefer not to put your finger in the pot, use a pencil. Sharpen the pencil to expose new wood, then insert it into the medium and twist it a few times. If the wood is damp, you don't need to water the plant.

Orchids without pseudobulbs or succulent leaves, such as paphiopedilums and phalaenopsis, should not be allowed to dry out completely between waterings. Test these

Fingers are excellent moisture meters, particularly for testing the moisture content of fine mixes such as those used for cymbidiums.

Watering Tips

The old expression "He who holds the hose, grows the rose" also applies to orchids, but only to the extent that proper watering is the key to success. Here are some suggestions to help you master this all-important aspect of orchid care.

☐ Just before you water a plant, lift the pot to see how much it weighs. With some practice, you will be able to tell whether the plant needs water simply by hefting it.

☐ Irrigate your plants in the morning so that the excess water will evaporate rapidly.

☐ All other things being equal, plants in clay pots or small pots will generally require water more often than will plants in plastic pots or large pots.

☐ You can tell if a pseudobulbous orchid is receiving enough water by looking at the pseudobulbs. The youngest pseudobulb should remain plump, but the older ones may shrink slightly between waterings without harm.

☐ As a potting medium ages, the air spaces in it shrink, making it retain more water. Thus, newly repotted plants need to be watered more often than those that have been in the same growing medium for a while.

---

plants before watering them as you would an epiphytic orchid, but water them when the medium is still slightly moist.

You will find that high temperatures, bright light, low humidity, and fast air movement will, singly or in combination, increase an orchid's need for water. By keeping an eye on your plants' growing conditions, you will learn how frequently they need water. Generally, you will probably find that you water most of your plants about once a week.

How to Water

When it's time to water an orchid, water it thoroughly. If possible, take the plant to the sink or bathtub and pour plenty of water through the potting medium. This thorough soaking will flush any accumulated salts out of the pot and will provide the even moisture that encourages large, healthy root systems. Use room-temperature water if possible—cold water may invigorate people, but it shocks plant roots and can damage the leaves of orchids such as phalaenopsis.

If the water in your area is hard—that is, full of dissolved minerals—flush the plants out with distilled water (or rainwater) every so often to keep the minerals from building up in the potting medium. Never use water that has been chemically softened—the sodium in this water will quickly kill the plants.

FERTILIZER

In the wild, epiphytic orchids obtain nutrients from the decaying organic debris that collects around their roots. Terrestrial orchids obtain nutrients from the organic matter on the ground. The plants do not absorb nutrients directly from organic matter; they depend on bacteria to break it down and liberate its constituents in simple forms the plants can readily absorb. As long as the temperature is warm enough to keep the bacteria active, they produce a continuous, dilute supply of nutrients.

Your orchids will grow best if you mimic this natural process by fertilizing them frequently with a dilute fertilizer solution. Luckily, you don't have to brew a concoction of dead leaves, bird droppings, and insect bodies to feed your plants—other equally effective and more convenient fertilizers are available.

Types of Fertilizers

Fertilizers may be organic (derived from plants and animals) or inorganic (derived from minerals). The nutrient content of both types is described by a set of three numbers on the fertilizer label. These numbers indicate the percentages of nitrogen, phosphorus, and potassium—in that order. For example, a fertilizer labeled 15-5-5 contains 15 percent nitrogen, 5 percent phosphorus, and 5 percent potassium. Some fertilizers also contain trace elements such as iron and zinc. These elements are just as important to healthy growth and flowering as nitrogen, phosphorus, and potassium; plants just need them in smaller quantities.

The type of fertilizer you choose depends mainly on the medium in which your plants are growing. Orchids growing in bark need much more nitrogen than phosphorus and potassium because the bark decays so rapidly. Although one would think the decaying bark would provide nitrogen for the plants, it actually does just the opposite. The bacteria that break down the bark take most of the nitrogen for their own use, leaving very little for the orchids. For this reason, orchids planted in bark should be fed with a fertilizer containing a high ratio of nitrogen to phosphorus and potassium, such as 30-10-10 or 15-5-5. Note that these formulations have the same ratios of nitrogen, phosphorus, and potassium (3:1:1). The first formulation is simply twice as concentrated. Fish emulsion labeled 5-1-1 is a popular organic fertilizer for orchids grown in a greenhouse, but its strong odor makes it unsuitable for home use.

Plants growing in tree fern fiber or other relatively stable materials do well with a balanced fertilizer such as 20-20-20 or 23-19-17. Balanced fertilizers are offered by many companies; the best contain iron and other trace elements.

Many growers alternate fertilizers, switching to a low nitrogen, high phosphorus fertilizer (such as 10-30-20) to stimulate flowering when the plants complete their vegetative growth. While not absolutely necessary, this practice may improve the quality and number of the flowers.

How to Fertilize

"Weekly, weakly" aptly describes the constant feeding regime that works best for orchids. It is also the easiest way to make sure your plants are adequately fed. Each time you water your plants, give them a half-strength fertilizer solution. (Half-strength is one half of the strength recommended on the label for houseplants.) If you have hard water, however, add fertilizer to the water every other time you water. The alternating plain waterings will flush excess minerals from the potting medium.

Fertilizer Tips

Most fertilizer problems result from too much rather than too little fertilizer. Keep in mind that in the wild, orchids grow in a very lean regime.

☐ If the tips of the leaves become dry and blackened, you may be overfertilizing. Cut off the burned tips with sterilized scissors, and pour plenty of fresh water through the medium to flush out the excess fertilizer. If the symptoms are severe, repot the plant with fresh medium.

☐ Don't fertilize plants suffering from too little water or damaged roots. Water them with plain water until they recover.

☐ Water plants immediately before fertilizing to prevent injury from fertilizer salts.

☐ Resist the urge to "push" your plants with extra fertilizer. Extra fertilizer actually stunts plants.

☐ Fertilize only when the plants are actively growing.

PROMOTING FLOWERING

Most orchids will flower on their own without any special treatment, as long as they are receiving adequate sunlight and proper temperatures. Some species, such as the deciduous dendrobiums, need seasonal treatments to promote flowering. These treatments usually involve cutting back on water and fertilizer to respect the plant's resting period—the period following a cycle of vegetative growth. It is impossible to say how long the resting treatment should last in terms of weeks or months—the requirements of the different species and the conditions under which they can be grown vary too much. Generally, you should allow the orchid to rest from the time its newest growth has matured until it starts to produce new growths or flower spikes. For specific recommendations on the rest requirements of orchids, look under the genus in question in the "Orchid Selection Guide," beginning on page 63.

CONTAINERS AND POTTING MEDIUMS

You will find that the type of container and growing medium you choose will have a great effect on how you care for your plants. Until you feel confident about your orchids' other growing conditions, keep things simple by using the kind of container and potting medium the plant or parent plant was growing in when you acquired it. Of course, if either has proved to be unsatisfactory or unavailable, you may want to change the type of container or potting medium.

Choosing the Right Container

Orchids are most often grown in plastic pots. Plastic pots are inexpensive, light in weight, absorb no toxic salts, and retain moisture. Some people prefer the natural look of unglazed clay. Porous clay pots allow the medium to dry out more quickly than it would in a plastic pot—an advantage if you are inclined to overwater. Stick with plastic, however, if you have hard water. The salts in hard water accumulate in the walls of clay pots and burn the roots.

The roots of some orchids, such as miniature oncidiums, cannot tolerate the moist conditions of a pot, but grow beautifully on slabs of cork, wood, tree fern fiber, or on branches

Opposite: In the wild, orchids are fertilized by a small but steady supply of decomposing leaves and other organic material. It doesn't take much to bring them into full bloom.

as in their natural habitats. Colonies of related species are often grown together on a slab for an enchanting display.

Choosing the Right Medium

Many potting mediums for orchids are available. Over the years, growers have tried everything from exotic fibers to common gravel. A tremendous variety of mixes has been concocted, ranging from simple mixtures of fir bark and perlite to elaborate combinations of up to seven ingredients. Despite the variety of mediums and mixtures, most orchid growers use fir bark alone or as the main ingredient in a mixture of materials. Commercially prepared mixes are also available; these may be the most convenient for the beginner.

Fir bark The most popular orchid potting material is fir bark. It is inexpensive, easy to handle, and the rough surfaces of the bark pieces supply the right combination of air and water to the roots.

Fir bark is available in three grades: fine, medium, and coarse. Fine bark (⅛- to ¼-inch pieces) is used for delicate seedlings or mericlones, or for mature plants with fine roots, such as miltonias. Medium bark (¼- to ½-inch pieces) is best for most epiphytic orchids. Coarse bark (½- to 1-inch pieces) is right for vandas and large phalaenopsis plants. Ungraded bark (with pieces of different sizes) should be avoided. The small pieces fill in the spaces between the large pieces, resulting in poor aeration.

Although fir bark can be used alone, many growers add coarse perlite to increase its water-holding capacity. Because perlite breaks

Fir bark

down much more slowly than bark, it also helps maintain aeration as the bark ages.

As soon as you put fir bark in a pot, it starts to break down. This is its main drawback. As the bark decays, the pieces shrink and settle in the container. As the pieces get smaller, the spaces between them get smaller too, causing the medium to hold more water and less air. Eventually, if the plant isn't repotted, the roots will rot. Generally, plants in medium and coarse fir bark need repotting every two years, but in humid, warm climates the bark breaks down rapidly and may need to be replaced annually. Fine fir bark generally lasts about a year, but in warm humid climates it breaks down too rapidly to be useful. For this reason, most orchid growers in Florida use tree fern fiber, a more stable medium.

The organisms responsible for the decay of bark use a great deal of nitrogen—a phenomenon known to horticulturists as "nitrogen draft." If there isn't enough nitrogen for the decay organisms and the plant, the plant suffers. You can't stop the decay, but you can easily compensate for it by using a high-nitrogen fertilizer. Most growers use a fertilizer containing a large percentage of nitrogen, such as 30-10-10, to fertilize plants potted in fir bark. (See Fertilizer, page 23.)

Gravel   Despite its advantage of absolute decay resistance, gravel is rarely used because it holds little water or nutrients, is very heavy, and can tear the roots from plants when they are eventually repotted. Plants growing in gravel need to be fertilized carefully and frequently; complete hydroponic fertilizer solutions are recommended.

Gravel

Lava rock   Plants growing in lava rock can remain undisturbed for many years, because lava does not decay. Lava is well aerated and retains water, though not as satisfactorily as fir bark. Its main disadvantage is its tendency to accumulate salts; don't use lava if your water contains large amounts of dissolved minerals. Lava is most commonly used in Hawaii, where its low cost and high resistance to decay make it the medium of preference. A fertilizer labeled 20-20-20 works well for plants growing in lava.

Lava rock

Man-made mediums   These include a variety of products made from clay or shale that has been fired to form nuggets of a porous material similar to lava rock. Like lava, expanded clay does not deteriorate, is well-aerated, and has excellent water-holding capacity. Unfortunately, it is expensive, difficult to obtain, and because of its weight, costly to ship. Expanded clay is most commonly used in Hawaii. Balanced fertilizers are recommended for man-made mediums.

Expanded shale

Perlite This processed volcanic material is used most often as an additive to other potting mediums. Perlite's low cost, high water-holding capacity, and decay resistance make it a popular additive to fir bark.

Perlite

Sphagnum moss This soft, spongy plant is found on the surface of bogs. It can retain up to 10 times its weight in water—far more than any other potting medium. It also contains an antiseptic that inhibits the "damping off" fungus disease of seedlings. Sphagnum comes in several forms: long or short fibers, alive or dried. Live sphagnum is best for orchids. It is green and, if not overwatered or over-fertilized, it will continue to live and grow after it is placed in the pot. It is used most often as an additive to other potting mediums, though some growers use it alone for special plants in small pots, or to nurse ailing plants back to health. Sphagnum sometimes contains a fungus that can infect people. This disease is very rare, but play it safe and always wear gloves when handling sphagnum.

Sphagnum moss

Cork Crushed cork is usually mixed in nearly equal parts with charcoal for potting orchids, and has a small but loyal following. Some say it lasts nearly three years; others say it rapidly breaks down to a slimy mess. The jury is still out.

Cork

Peat moss When sphagnum moss dies and sinks into a bog, it breaks down slowly to form peat moss. Peat moss has an even greater water-holding capacity than sphagnum, but it decomposes more rapidly. Coarse peat, commonly called poultry peat because of its use on the floors of chicken coops, was once a favorite ingredient in orchid mixes, but it has become scarce and expensive and is now rarely used as a principal ingredient in potting mixes. It should not be mixed with tree fern, cork, or osmunda, but may be blended with fir bark or charcoal. Coarse peat moss contains few nutrients and breaks down slowly, so balanced fertilizers are recommended. Horticultural peat, though less expensive and widely available, is too fine and dense for potting orchids.

Peat moss

Osmunda fiber   These fibers are the roots of ferns in the genus *Osmunda*. It used to be the most popular medium for orchid culture, but it has become so expensive that hardly anyone uses it anymore. Fir bark seems to work just as well, is easier to handle, and is much less expensive.

Osmunda fiber

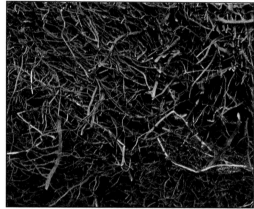

Tree fern   The second most popular potting medium for orchids is tree fern fiber. Its resistance to decay and excellent aeration make it the preferred medium in Florida, where the year-round warm temperatures and high humidity quickly turn a pot of fir bark into a soggy mess.

The disadvantages of tree fern are its relatively high cost and low water retention; tree fern costs about twice as much as fir bark and needs to be watered twice as often. To overcome these problems, many tree fern users mix in some coarse fir bark to stretch both their dollars and the intervals between waterings.

Tree fern

Because tree fern breaks down so slowly, you don't need to use a high-nitrogen fertilizer. Balanced fertilizers labeled 23-19-17 or 20-20-20 supply a well-rounded ration.

Redwood bark   Similar to fir bark, redwood bark offers the advantage of decay resistance. Though it comes from California, most redwood bark is used in Florida, where it lasts even longer than tree fern. Unfortunately, it also costs a little more than tree fern. It is often used as a component in mixtures. A balanced fertilizer is best for plants growing in redwood bark.

Redwood bark

Charcoal   Hardwood charcoal (not pressed powder briquettes) is added most often to cork or redwood bark, both of which produce a lot of acid. Charcoal is referred to as a "sweetener" because it absorbs the acids. It is also a common component of commercially packaged mixes. Like lava, charcoal collects salts—don't use it if you have hard water.

Charcoal

REPOTTING

Sooner or later, each of your orchids will need to be repotted. Orchids may need repotting for a variety of reasons. Like other houseplants, they need to be moved to larger pots as they grow. More frequently, the growing medium decays and begins to restrict the flow of air to the roots before the plant has outgrown its container. In this case, the plant is repotted with fresh medium back into its original container, or into a new one of the same size. Also, repotting can be the first step in nursing an overwatered plant back to health.

When to Repot

Unless you are trying to save a sick or damaged orchid, wait to repot it until just after flowering, the time most orchids begin a cycle of root growth. Orchids repotted at this stage are quick to reestablish in the new medium and are also easy to handle. The new roots in sympodial orchids are usually very obvious. In some types, they appear at the base of the new growths when the shoot is a couple of inches long. In others, the roots begin to grow from the newest part of the plant before the new shoot appears. In either case, you want to re pot the plant when the new roots are just beginning to appear. Once the roots have grown more than ½ inch, they are easily broken during transplanting. Although mature roots may quickly branch and continue to grow if broken off, young roots don't resume growth for an entire season if they are damaged.

The new roots are not as readily apparent in monopodial orchids such as phalaenopsis, but they usually begin growing as soon as the plant finishes flowering. Like the sympodials, monopodial orchids should be repotted when the new roots are less than ½ inch long.

How to Repot

If you've learned to repot your other houseplants carefully without breaking up the ball of soil and roots, you may be surprised by the techniques used in repotting orchids. When you repot an orchid, you must remove all the growing medium from the roots, leaving them bare and looking very vulnerable. This may seem to be an overly drastic treatment, but if you don't remove all the mix from the roots, it will continue to decay and could eventually lead to root rot.

You will need a sharp knife with a long blade, a pair of pruning shears, a blunt dowel or stick, and, of course, the potting mix. If you are using a clay pot, you will also need some broken crockery to cover the drainage hole. It is very important that you sterilize all cutting tools to prevent the spread of viruses. Sterilize the cutting tool before working on each plant by holding the blade in a flame for several seconds. A butane lighter works well.

If you are using fir bark or tree fern fiber, soak it overnight in tub of water. By morning, the sawdust and very small pieces that might clog the mix will have separated from the larger pieces and settled to the bottom. Use the floating pieces to pot the orchid.

1. Water the orchid A thorough watering makes the roots easier to handle.

2. Remove the plant from the pot Lay the pot on its side, grasp the plant at the base and

Orchids should be repotted before the new roots grow more than ½ inch long. In many sympodial orchids, new roots emerge from the youngest growths before the new shoots appear. A new shoot will soon sprout from the base of the front pseudobulb of this plant.

tug gently. The root ball of a terrestrial will usually slide right out, but the roots of epiphytes often cling tenaciously to the container. If the plant won't come out with a gentle tug, turn it back upright and work a sharp, long-bladed knife around the inside of the pot, between the pot and the roots. Then turn the pot back on its side, grasp the root ball as before, and gently tug the plant out of the pot. If it still won't come out—which is sometimes the case with cymbidiums in clay pots—break the pot by tapping on it lightly with a hammer.

3. Clean the roots Gently shake the old potting medium from the roots. Wash away the clinging bits with a stream of water. Cut off any rotten roots with sterilized pruning shears. (Rotten roots are black or dark brown; some portions may have sloughed away leaving only the threadlike center.) Leave the healthy roots intact unless they have grown outside the pot and would be broken off in repotting; if this is the case, cut them back to 3 or 4 inches.

4. Divide the plant This is optional. If the plant is growing in a fine, symmetrical pattern and is producing new growth from several points, you won't want to divide it because it is on the way to becoming a spectacular specimen. But if it has grown in a straight line across the pot, died out in the center, or has some other defect, improve its appearance and stimulate new growth by dividing it. You may also want to divide the plant in order to propagate it. (To maximize the number of plants propagated by division, see page 35.) The techniques for dividing sympodial orchids are different from those used for monopodial orchids; be sure to follow the instructions pertaining to the type of orchid you have (see illustration on page 31).

Sympodials To divide a sympodial, cut it into sections by slicing through the rhizome (the horizontal stem joining the pseudobulbs) with a sterile knife or shears. Leave at least three leafy growths per section, preferably four or five. Remove and discard the leafless, shriveled pseudobulbs, but leave the healthy ones intact—these are needed because they supply food to the rest of the plant and may sprout new growth.

Remove the Plant From the Pot

Clean and Trim the Roots

Rotted roots

Paphiopedilums don't have pseudobulbs, but their growths are connected by a rhizome. Thus, you divide a paphiopedilum in the same manner as you would a sympodial with pseudobulbs, cutting through the rhizome to create divisions with at least three leafy growths each, as described at left.

Monopodials Shorten a leggy monopodial by cutting off the top of the plant just below a node with well-developed aerial roots. If new growths have sprouted from the base of the old stem, cut off the old stem. Otherwise repot the old stem—it will usually produce new growths at the top which can later be removed and planted.

5. Choose a pot The pot for a sympodial should be large enough to accommodate two years of new growth between the youngest

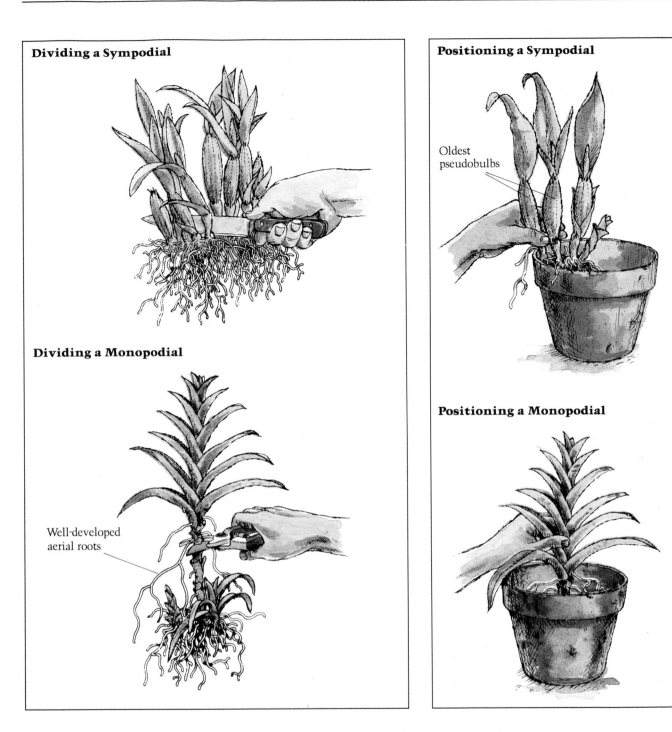

Dividing a Sympodial

Dividing a Monopodial

Well-developed aerial roots

Positioning a Sympodial

Oldest pseudobulbs

Positioning a Monopodial

pseudobulbs and the rim. To test for size, hold the plant in a pot with the oldest pseudobulbs against the rim and see how much room there is in front of the youngest shoot. You want to choose the smallest pot that will still allow two years of growth—most orchids grow and bloom best when relatively potbound. Pots for monopodials should also be on the small side; pick one just large enough to accommodate the roots without bending or breaking them.

6. Pot the plant Arrange several pot shards over the drainage hole in the bottom of a clay pot (plastic pots with several small drainage holes don't need shards). Put a few inches of bark on top of the shards. Because they grow in different directions, sympodials and monopodials are potted differently; follow the instructions pertaining to the type of orchid you are repotting.

Sympodials Hold the plant in position with the oldest pseudobulbs against the rim. Adjust the height of the plant in the pot so that the base of the rhizome is about ½ inch below the rim. If the new growths are higher than the old pseudobulbs, position the plant at

Tamping Bark Around the Roots

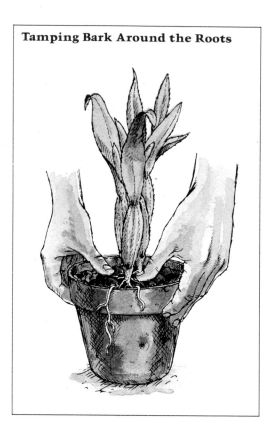

Supporting the Plant

an angle so that the new growths are growing parallel to the bottom of the pot. This will keep the plant from climbing as it grows. Fill in bark around the roots, firmly tamping it in with your fingers or the dowel. After adding a few handfuls, lift the pot and thump it back down to settle the bark. Continue adding bark until it covers the sides of the rhizome. Thump the pot again.

Monopodials Center the plant in the pot. You want to position the plant so the bottom of the lowest leaf is at the surface of the bark—about ½ inch below the rim of the pot. If the lowest leaf doesn't have at least three healthy roots on the stem below it, strip off one or more of the bottom leaves until there are healthy roots that you can anchor in the bark. Cut off the very bottom of the stem if it doesn't have roots on it. Fill in bark around the roots, gently tamping it in with your fingers or the dowel. After each handful, thump the bottom of the pot against the table to settle the bark. Continue adding bark until it reaches the bottom of the lowest leaf. Thump the pot again.

7. Support the plant Top-heavy orchids such as cattleyas need to be supported with a stake to keep them from toppling. Other orchids with large root systems can stand on their own. Metal stakes that are clipped to the side of the pot work best. Clip the stake to the pot next to the back of the plant and tie the pseudobulbs to it with string. Rhizome clips designed to anchor the plant in the medium are also available from orchid supply companies (see Sources, page 61).

Although small containers are best for the health of the roots, they may appear out of scale with the plant and also might tip over easily. Improve both the visual balance and the stability of the plant by placing the pot inside a larger pot and filling in the space around the sides and bottom with gravel.

Post-Planting Care

When you finish potting and staking, move the plant to a slightly shadier location than where it grew before. Make sure the air is adequately humid, but withhold water for one to two weeks to give the cut surfaces of the roots and stems a chance to heal. Water the plant less frequently than usual for the next two months to stimulate root growth, and fertilize it lightly when you water it. After four to six weeks you can gradually move the orchid back into brighter light and begin to treat it as usual.

Opposite: It's an axiom of orchid growing that a collection will expand to fill all available space. Many mail-order orchid nurseries were started by hobbyists who, after several years of dividing and repotting their plants, simply ran out of room.

Potting Tips

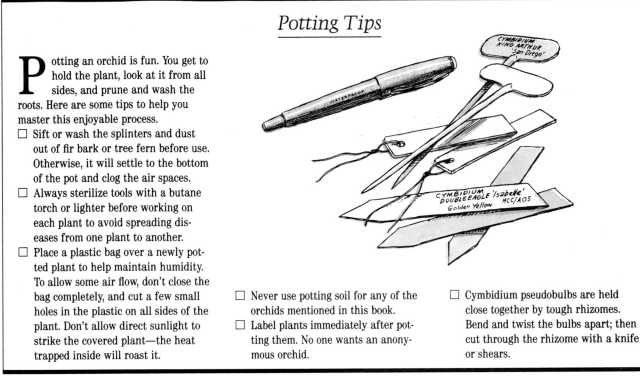

Potting an orchid is fun. You get to hold the plant, look at it from all sides, and prune and wash the roots. Here are some tips to help you master this enjoyable process.

☐ Sift or wash the splinters and dust out of fir bark or tree fern before use. Otherwise, it will settle to the bottom of the pot and clog the air spaces.

☐ Always sterilize tools with a butane torch or lighter before working on each plant to avoid spreading diseases from one plant to another.

☐ Place a plastic bag over a newly potted plant to help maintain humidity. To allow some air flow, don't close the bag completely, and cut a few small holes in the plastic on all sides of the plant. Don't allow direct sunlight to strike the covered plant—the heat trapped inside will roast it.

☐ Never use potting soil for any of the orchids mentioned in this book.

☐ Label plants immediately after potting them. No one wants an anonymous orchid.

☐ Cymbidium pseudobulbs are held close together by tough rhizomes. Bend and twist the bulbs apart; then cut through the rhizome with a knife or shears.

Forming a Pad of Sphagnum Moss

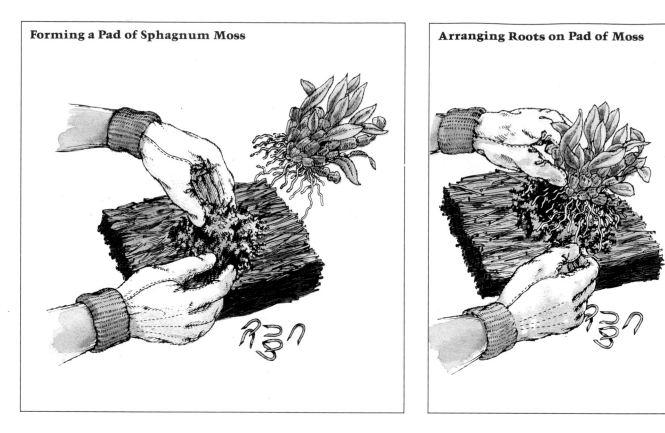

Arranging Roots on Pad of Moss

Transplanting Orchids Onto Slabs of Wood, Cork, or Tree Fern

Orchids are attached to slabs with twine, wire, or staples. Electrician's staples work well; their flat tops make them easy to press into the wood or cork, and it doesn't take long for a layer of rust to blend them into the background. In addition to staples, you'll need a slab, some sphagnum moss, and pliers. Always wear gloves when handling sphagnum.

Start by making a small, slim pad (about the same diameter as the plant) out of the sphagnum moss. Staple the pad to the slab and put the plant on top of it, arranging the roots so they extend outwards. Fasten the roots to the slab, putting small rolled-up pieces of moss between them and the staples or wire. In very humid or wet conditions, attach the plants directly to the slab without the pad of moss. Keep the plants lightly shaded and water them infrequently until they become established; this usually takes six to eight weeks.

Most slabs last a very long time; you won't need to transplant the orchids until they begin to hang off the sides. Even then, if the slab is still in good condition, you can allow the plants to continue growing undisturbed by attaching the overgrown slab to the center of a larger one of the same material.

Fastening Roots to Slab With Staples

PROPAGATING ORCHIDS

An orchid seed is tiny, about the size of a speck of dust. Millions of seeds are contained in a single seed pod, but in nature only a few ever find the right conditions to grow into mature plants. In producing new hybrids, orchid breeders shift the odds to favor the seeds by sprouting them in sterile conditions on a special nutrient jelly. This is expensive and time-consuming work; luckily there are simpler and more reliable ways to propagate orchids. Orchids can be propagated vegetatively by dividing mature plants, planting offshoots, or (on a commercial scale) through tissue culture.

Division

Many orchids are easily propagated by division, a process of splitting a plant into two or more actively growing pieces at repotting time. In the repotting section (beginning on page 29) are instructions for producing a few large divisions. When propagating, however, you usually want to produce as many new plants as possible, so the techniques are a little different.

To propagate sympodial orchids by division, start by following the directions for repotting: Divide the plants into portions containing a minimum of three leafy pseudobulbs and plant these divisions in separate pots. In this case, however, don't discard the dormant pseudobulbs you removed from the active growths; these can be used to make new plants. Strip away the old leaf bases if present and plant the pseudobulbs in moist sphagnum moss or fine bark with the "eyes" (dormant buds) above the surface of the medium. Place them in a warm area and keep the moss or bark moist but not soggy. When the buds sprout new growths, gradually acclimate them to the growing conditions of the mature plants. They will reach blooming size in one to three years.

Offshoots

Offshoots, commonly called keikis (their Hawaiian name, pronounced "key-keys"), are small plants produced at the base or along the stems of monopodials, or from the pseudobulbs of some sympodials. The leaves of the keikis form first, followed by the roots. When the roots are 1 to 2 inches long, twist or cut the keikis off and plant them separately in

Sympodial With Offshoots Emerging From Base of Pseudobulb

Monopodial With Offshoots Emerging From Base of Older Plant

Phalaenopsis Plant With Keikis

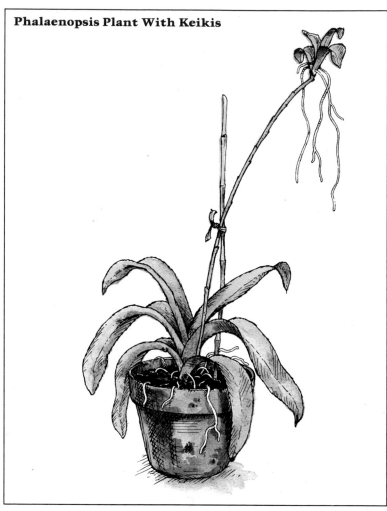

In the brave new world of commercial orchid production, most plants begin their lives in flasks of nutrient solution. In this laboratory, the flasks are agitated on rotating wheels. Other types of spinners and shakers are used, but all of them are designed to jostle the embryos and aerate the nutrient solution.

fine bark. Under good conditions, they will reach flowering size within two years.

Phalaenopsis plants sprout keikis from buds along the flower stem. These can be removed from the plant when they have well-developed roots and treated as other types of keikis. If the roots aren't coming along, bend the flower stems down and plant the keikis in a pot of bark. Once the keikis have rooted into the bark, cut them free from the flower stems.

Meristem Cloning

The techniques described above work well on a small scale, but they are far too limited for commercial growers who need to produce as many plants as possible—as quickly as possible—from a single superior specimen. Meristem cloning (usually shortened to "mericloning" or "meristemming") lets growers rapidly produce hundreds of plants from a single shoot. Without this tissue culture technique, fine orchids would still be rare and very expensive. Although mericloning is complicated and expensive, the basics are fascinating and worth knowing—most hybrid plants start out as tiny lumps of tissue swirling in flasks of sterile nutrient solution.

Suppose an orchid breeder has painstakingly nurtured a hundred seedlings from a cross and found—years after the flower was pollinated—that one of the offspring has spectacular flowers. In addition to being beautiful, this new hybrid is valuable—valuable enough that the grower will go to a great deal of trouble to propagate it for sale.

To start the process, the plant is taken to a very clean laboratory where the tip of one of the shoots is removed. Working with a scalpel and microscope in a chamber designed to exclude airborne fungi and bacteria, a technician carefully strips the embryonic leaves away from this shoot tip. The tiny leaves are removed from the shoot tip to reveal the meristem, a primal lump of actively growing cells less than ½ millimeter in diameter. Meristems are like embryos, capable of growing and changing into the cells that form leaves, stems, roots, and eventually, flowers.

The meristem is placed in a flask of nutrient solution and put in a climate-controlled chamber where it is gently agitated by a machine. The lump grows other lumps, which are removed and placed in other flasks. These

These young plants are ready to be weaned from the bottle and exposed to the relatively harsher conditions of a greenhouse. Flasks of plantlets are available from some nurseries, but the tiny plants are difficult to grow.

lumps generate more lumps, which are also removed. This process of orchid fission continues until hundreds—sometimes thousands—of embryonic orchids are swirling in flasks. When enough lumps have been produced, they are planted in flasks of solid nutrient medium. There they develop into tiny plants with leaves, stems, and roots. Eventually the plants grow large enough to be transplanted out into the open air. Several years later, these clones may be found flowering on windowsills and in greenhouses throughout the world.

Growing Plants From Flasks

Some nurseries offer flasks of orchid seedlings growing in nutrient jelly. Although these tiny plants are inexpensive, they are also very tender and difficult to grow even for a veteran orchid grower. But if you have a greenhouse and think you would enjoy the challenge, you can find the methods for transplanting and growing seedlings from flasks in *Home Orchid Growing* by Rebecca Northen.

PROBLEMS

Orchids are tough plants, resistant to pests and diseases and capable of enduring a considerable amount of environmental stress. But if a plant's natural defenses are weakened by adverse growing conditions, it may succumb

to insects or diseases. The key to growing healthy orchids is to avoid stressing them.

As it turns out, most orchid stress is related to water—either too much or too little. Too much water on the roots, caused by overwatering or a poor growing medium, makes them rot. Too little water on the roots (or in the air) stresses the plants, and stressed plants are an invitation to scales, mealybugs, and other insects. If the leaves aren't washed occasionally, populations of spider mites may explode on their dusty surfaces. Leaves and flowers can't tolerate long periods of wetness; standing water encourages infection by bacteria and fungi.

This may appear to be a no-win situation, but keep in mind that these are just the extremes; many orchids can withstand long periods of drought without being harmed, and if they are growing in the proper growing medium they will tolerate a great deal of moisture.

Aside from minimizing stress, you can also prevent problems by keeping the growing area and plants clean. Fungi form millions of spores on dead leaves and flowers, so cut dead material off the plants as soon as you notice it. The papery sheath on pseudobulbs provides a perfect hiding place for scales and mealybugs. Leave the sheaths on new growths, but remove them as soon as they dry out and peel away from the surface of the pseudobulb. Remove dead leaf tips with sharp scissors or shears, making the cut about ¼ inch into the healthy tissue. Flame the shears between plants to avoid transmitting virus diseases.

Diagnosing Problems

Your first step in diagnosing a problem is to make sure you know what kind of growing conditions the plant prefers. Then, while you are inspecting the plant, compare what it needs to what it has been getting. In this way, you will often be able to predict a symptom before you even find it.

A magnifying glass will come in handy for finding small insects such as mites and scale crawlers. (When the plant recovers, use the glass to enjoy the details of the flowers.) In some cases, you'll need to inspect the roots of an ailing plant. Before you take the plant out of the pot, make sure you have enough fresh medium to repot it, if necessary.

Overwatering/pot too large

Plant overgrown

Underwatering/insufficient humidity

Overfertilization

PROBLEMS CAUSED BY IMPROPER CULTURE

Symptoms	Possible Cause	Treatment
Pseudobulbs (and leaves, if succulent) shrivel, growth slows or stops. Plant is loose in pot; inspection of roots reveals rot.	Overwatering.	Reduce watering, or repot if potting medium has decayed (see page 29). Keep plant in shaded, humid area until new roots establish.
	Pot is too large or medium has decomposed.	Repot the plant (see page 29).
Same as above, but roots are firm and white.	Underwatering.	Water the plant thoroughly, several times in succession until medium is soaked. Pseudobulbs should plump up in a day or two. Water more frequently to prevent further stress.
	Insufficient humidity.	Increase humidity (see page 19).
Tips or edges of leaves are burned. Roots are withered, especially at the tips. No mineral deposits are found on the pot or medium.	Overfertilization.	Leach out fertilizer by pouring several gallons of deionized water through the growing medium. (See page 23 for information on how to fertilize orchids.)
Gradual, even yellowing of the leaves; oldest leaves are affected first. Foliage is dull. New growth is stunted. Pseudobulbs extend out over edges of pot.	Plant is overgrown; pot is too small.	Transplant to larger pot or divide plant.

Too little light

Air pollution/temperature fluctuation

High concentration of minerals

Too much light

PROBLEMS CAUSED BY IMPROPER CULTURE

Symptoms	Possible Cause	Treatment
Scaly mineral deposits are found on pot and on surface of medium. Leaf tips are burned, new growth is stunted.	Water contains high concentrations of minerals, and may not be added to pot in quantities sufficient to flush the salts out of the growing medium.	Pour several gallons of deionized water through growing medium to leach out salts, or repot the plant. If water is extremely hard, mix it with deionized water or rainwater.
Scorched blotches on leaves and exposed surfaces of pseudobulbs, or general yellowing. Flower buds may be deformed.	Sunburn, too much light.	Provide less light, lower daytime temperature, or increase humidity and air movement.
Foliage is dark green and healthy, but plant won't flower.	Too little light.	Increase light gradually over a period of at least a month. If plant is growing under fluorescent lights, add wide-spectrum bulbs (see page 46), raise the plants closer to the bulbs, or increase the time the lights are on.
Flower damage, ranging from drying and discoloring of the tips of the sepals to rapid wilting of the entire flower. Buds may stop developing or fall off. Sheaths may yellow and dry up before buds appear.	Ethylene or sulfur dioxide air pollution from smog, pilot lights, stove, or heater.	Improve ventilation. Make sure gas appliances are adjusted properly.
	Temperature fluctuation. Large and rapid changes in temperature are a common cause of bud drop.	Keep temperatures within prescribed limits for the type of orchid. (See "Orchid Selection Guide," beginning on page 63.)

Inadequate watering

Too few hours of darkness

PROBLEMS CAUSED BY IMPROPER CULTURE

Symptoms	Possible Cause	Treatment
New leaves of *Miltonia* (or other thin-leaved orchids) emerge pleated.	Inadequate watering; growing medium dries out too much between waterings.	Water plant more often. Keep medium moist (but not soggy).
Plants under lights have healthy growth and proper leaf color, but won't flower.	Too few hours of darkness, or no resting period.	Turn the lights off for eight hours per night. Observe plant's resting period as required.

PROBLEMS CAUSED BY PESTS

Symptoms	Pest	Treatment
Fine stippling on the undersides of the leaves, sometimes on the buds and flowers, creating a dull, silvery effect. Fine webbing may be visible. Growth slows or stops.	Spider mites. Microscopic yellow, green, or red mites are found on lower surfaces of leaves with a magnifying glass.	Wash foliage with warm water and a mild liquid detergent. Take plants outside and spray them with dicofol. Treat plants once a week for several weeks to kill the mites as they hatch. To avoid introducing mites to your collection, inspect new plants carefully. Mites thrive in dust; keep foliage clean to prevent further infestation.
Buds, flowers, and tender new growth are pitted or stunted. Tiny insects often visible. A sticky fluid secreted by the insects provides a medium for growth of sooty mold (a black fungus) and attracts ants.	Aphids. Small (less than ⅛ inch), soft-bodied green, yellow, or pink insects cluster on the new growth, flowers, or flower buds. Cymbidiums are especially susceptible.	For small infestations, washing the plant with warm water and a mild detergent often suffices. For bigger problems, spray with malathion or Orthene Systemic Insect Control®. Sooty mold can be wiped off the leaves. Ants, if present, won't harm orchids, but they do carry other insects from plant to plant; if necessary, control them with a household spray, but don't use it on the orchids.
Fuzzy white masses appearing on the leaves, in the clefts between them, and on the pseudobulbs, particularly at their bases and under the sheaths.	Mealybugs. Fringed insects up to ¼ inch long with a white powdery or waxy covering.	Remove mealybugs with a cotton swab soaked in alcohol. Carefully search crevices, folds, and other hidden areas of the plant. If necessary, spray with malathion, Orthene Systemic Insect Control® or diazinon. Add a wetting agent (usually called a spreader-sticker) to the spray to break the waxy barrier on the insects.
Leaves are disfigured by broad scars and holes. Root tips are missing. Trails of shiny, dried mucus may be found on the plants and containers.	Snails and slugs. Many kinds of snails and slugs feed on orchid leaves and roots. Although not a common problem indoors, they may come in on plants that have been outside or in a greenhouse.	Pick them off. Search carefully; small ones hide in bark or under leaves during the day. Baits are effective, but are usually not necessary indoors.

Spider mites

Scales

Aphids

Snails and slugs

Mealybugs

PROBLEMS CAUSED BY PESTS

Symptoms	Pest	Treatment
Elliptical or round bumps, 1/10 to 1/3 inch long, attached to leaves, stems, pseudobulbs, and flowers. When severe, the plant may be scarred and stunted. A sticky fluid secreted from the bumps may provide a medium for growth of sooty mold (a black fungus) or attract ants.	Scales. The bumps are the shells of the scales, which are legless insects that suck sap from the plant. Several types of scales attack orchids.	Remove scales with a swab soaked in alcohol. Inspect plants often, removing scales as you find them. Control severe infestations by taking plants outdoors and spraying them with malathion. Malathion is most effective against the tiny young scales (crawlers), which have no shells and can move about the plant or from one plant to another. Spray the plants weekly for several weeks to kill the crawlers as they hatch.

Black rot fungus   *Root rot fungus*

PROBLEMS CAUSED BY DISEASES

Symptoms	Disease	Treatment
Soft, rotted areas begin in leaves or new growth, spread down into rhizome and roots, then upward into other leaves if not checked. Infected leaf areas initially are purplish brown, turning black; advancing edges are yellowish.	Black rot fungus, *Phytophthora cactorum* or *Pythium ultimum*. Cattleyas and phalaenopsis are especially susceptible, but oncidiums, dendrobiums, and vandas also get the disease.	Cut off infected areas ½ inch into healthy tissue. Sterilize the cutting tool in flame after each cut. Take plant outside and drench with a solution of Natriphene®, Truban™, or copper sulfate. Isolate plant in a low-humidity area and allow it to dry off. Water carefully until plant recovers.
Plant wilts because roots have rotted. Brown rotten areas may extend from roots into rhizomes. Leaves become yellowed and twisted.	Root rot fungus, *Fusarium oxysporum cattleyae* or *Rhizoctonia solani*.	Repot the plant, using new medium and a sterile pot. Cut off all rotted roots and discolored rhizomes, sterilizing the blade between cuts. Take the plant outside and drench with a fungicide containing benomyl.
Sunken, water-soaked lesion on leaf, which eventually turns brown or black. Lesion exudes dark liquid.	Bacterial brown spot, *Pseudomonas cattleyae*. Most common disease of phalaenopsis, but infects other orchids as well.	Remove badly infected leaves. Take plant outside and spray with RD20® (¼–½ tablespoon per gallon of water). Exudate contains bacteria; isolate plant to keep disease from spreading. Discard plant if disease spreads to crown.
Leaves have sunken, purplish brown or black spots. Spots start as yellow areas on leaf undersides, becoming visible on both sides of leaf as they darken.	Leaf spot fungus such as *Cercospora* or *Colletotrichum*.	Take plant outdoors and spray with a fungicide containing benomyl. Remove badly damaged leaves. Leaves with a few spots may be left on plant. It's a rare orchid that doesn't have a spot or two.
Small, circular tan or pinkish spots appear on sepals or petals of flowers.	Petal blight, *Botrytis cinerea*. Usually only a problem in humid greenhouses.	Cut off and destroy all spotted flowers. Increase air circulation and lower humidity, if possible. Clean up any decaying plant matter in area that may harbor the fungus. Avoid splashing flowers when watering plants.

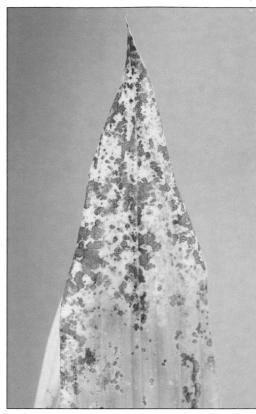

Leaf spot fungus

Petal blight

Bacterial brown spot

Virus

PROBLEMS CAUSED BY DISEASES

Symptoms	Disease	Treatment
Black, red, or yellow spots or streaks appear on leaves. Flowers may have white or brown streaks or mosaic patterns.	Virus. Many virus diseases infect orchids, but diagnosis can be difficult; virus symptoms often resemble other less serious problems.	Have plant tested to confirm diagnosis (see Sources, page 61). Plant viruses are incurable; destroy infected plants. Plants may carry viruses without showing symptoms, so always sterilize tools before use on each plant.

Special Growing Areas

Special growing areas such as greenhouses and artificial-light gardens provide ideal conditions for raising orchids.

Although a sunny windowsill is the easiest place to start an orchid collection, lack of sunlight doesn't have to keep you from growing orchids. Artificial lights will brighten a marginally sunny windowsill, illuminate a bookshelf growing area, or transform a windowless basement into a tropical wonderland of show-quality orchids.

In some ways, artificial lights are better than sunlight for orchids. Grown in the sun, few plants have unblemished leaves; grown under lights, plants can have perfect foliage. The cool glow of the lights can't burn the leaves, and the plants grow more symmetrically because the light comes from directly overhead. Also, the constant intensity of the lights ensures that the leaves will all be approximately the same size no matter what time of year they are produced.

Ready-made light gardens for orchids are available. Glass cases with built-in lights, fans, and heaters provide the best climate control, but you pay a large price for a small growing area. Multitiered stands and carts with built-in humidity trays and fluorescent lights are offered in a variety of sizes and provide an easy and effective solution to a lack of light. Simple units consisting of a fluorescent fixture and frame are designed to illuminate a small table or shelf.

If you are a do-it-yourselfer, you will find it is not difficult to build your own light garden with the components offered by lighting supply stores and mail-order suppliers. See Sources, page 61, for the addresses of companies that specialize in indoor gardening equipment.

Although many popular species and hybrids do well in the home, a much greater variety of orchids will grow in the bright, moist climate of a greenhouse.

CHOOSING THE RIGHT SPOT

You probably have several places in your home suitable for growing orchids under lights. If your garden is near a window, you may not need as many light bulbs and the plants will respond well to the natural light. By using a basement, stairwell, or other out-of-the-way place, you also can create a growing area without sacrificing any of your living space. The concrete floors and walls of most basements are normally unharmed by humidity or a little water. Some growers line the walls and ceilings of their basement growing areas with plastic to maintain the humidity. If the basement has no windows, a fan or two will take care of the plants' need for air movement. In choosing a suitable place, remember that you will need electrical outlets for the artificial lights. A nearby sink is also convenient.

TYPES OF LIGHTS

Fluorescent lights—the tubes used in offices and classrooms—turn electricity into light more efficiently than do the incandescent lights used in homes. Efficiency in lighting mainly refers to the amount of heat given off by the bulbs or fixtures. This property becomes important when you are illuminating orchids, which need to be very close to the bulbs in order to receive enough light to bloom. To keep the plants from burning, incandescent bulbs must be placed at least one foot from the foliage; however, at this distance, the light isn't bright enough to make them flower so fluorescent tubes are preferred.

Fluorescent Lights

The tubular glass bulb of a fluorescent lamp is coated on the inside with a mixture of phosphorescent chemicals called phosphor and then filled with a gas. When the light is turned on, the electrodes at the ends of the tube cause a current to flow through the gas, which emits high-energy radiation. This radiation is absorbed by the phosphor and re-emitted as visible light. Most of the light comes out of the center of the tube; the brightness drops off dramatically near the ends.

The type of phosphor used in the tube determines the color of the light given off by the lamp. "Cool white" lamps—the kind commonly used in offices—emit most of their light

in the blue part of the spectrum. This is fine for writing memos and talking on the phone, or even for growing healthy foliage, but plants also need red light in order to flower. At first, indoor gardeners solved this problem by adding incandescent lights to provide the red wavelengths, but the heat produced by the incandescent bulbs in such arrangements has always been a problem. In response to the demand for fluorescent light that will make plants flower, manufacturers developed special bulbs that produced light in the red and the blue parts of the spectrum. But some of them left out the middle—the yellow and green. The predominance of red and blue light emitted from these bulbs distorts the colors of the plants growing under them. Reds are vivid, yellows glow brightly, and pinks pop with phosphorescent intensity, but the foliage looks dull and unattractive.

Full-spectrum bulbs, now available from a number of companies, emit light with a spectral distribution approaching that of sunlight. These bulbs give a more natural rendering of plant colors while producing the wavelengths required for growth and flowering. Trade names include Tru-Bloom®, Naturescent®, Gro-Lux WS®, and Vita-Lite®. (The Vita-Lite Powertwist® bulb is brighter than a standard tube because its twist construction gives the

Orchids, African violets, and other plants thrive under full-spectrum fluorescent lights. Mirrors reflect the light emitted toward the sides of the fixtures back onto the plants.

A basement doesn't have to be a dark, dingy place. A cart-type light garden provides plenty of illumination for orchids and other flowering plants, and can be set up practically anywhere.

phosphor a greater surface area.) These bulbs come in a variety of lengths and wattages, and have standard two-pin connectors.

Fluorescent fixtures Of all the fixtures on the market, the best for lighting orchids are made of aluminum. Aluminum fixtures are superior to steel because they resist corrosion and conduct heat away from the unit most effectively. A fixture that is going to be the plant's only source of light should hold four bulbs. Two-bulb fixtures will suffice for supplementing natural light, or they can be paired to simulate a four-bulb fixture. Although fixtures as short as 18 inches are available, the minimum length for orchid growing is 48 inches; shorter lamps don't produce enough light and are much less efficient. You will find, when considering all these factors, that the best fixtures for orchid growing are 48 inches long (or longer), hold four bulbs, and are made of aluminum. A fixture of this size will illuminate a 2-foot by 4-foot area—enough space for about 30 orchid plants.

In addition to holding the bulbs, the fixture houses a ballast, a transformer that regulates the power to the bulbs. Ballasts vary in quality; the better they are, the less power they use, the less heat they produce, and the longer they last. Some suppliers allow you to select your ballasts when you order your fixtures. Electronic ballasts are the coolest and most efficient, but are also the most expensive. Choose an electronic ballast when heat is a problem in your growing area or if your electricity is particularly expensive.

It is difficult to estimate the cost of running a fluorescent fixture. Your cost will vary depending on the type of ballast you choose, the cost of your electricity, how long the lights are on, and the temperature in the growing area. You can assume, though, that it will cost anywhere from $2 to $5 a month to run a two-bulb, 40-watt, 48-inch fixture.

Other Kinds of Lights

Mercury vapor, high-power sodium, and quartz lamps are much brighter than fluorescent lamps, but they are also much more expensive to purchase and maintain. Their chief advantage is brightness—a quartz lamp is bright enough to sustain orchids with light requirements that can't be met with fluorescent light. Because they are so bright (and hot) they are placed farther from the plants, and can thus illuminate tall plants that would not fit under fluorescent fixtures. These lights require special fixtures that must be installed by an electrician. They can be purchased from most indoor gardening suppliers.

GROWING ORCHIDS UNDER LIGHTS

Growing orchids under lights is similar to growing them on a windowsill—their requirements for light, humidity, water, and fertilizer are the same. In this case, though, you adjust the amount of light the plant receives by adjusting its distance from the light bulbs and by varying the length of time the lights are turned on.

Maximizing Light Intensity

Do everything you can to maximize the light intensity for your plants—you can't overexpose them to fluorescent light. Use fixtures with reflectors. Paint the walls and other surfaces in the growing area with flat white paint, or apply stick-on mirror tiles. If your growing area doubles as a display, consider placing a large mirror behind the plants to reflect light into the foliage and give you another view of the flowers.

Most beginners place their plants too far from the light bulbs. A few inches can make a world of difference: A plant 2 feet from a light bulb only receives one fourth the light of a plant 1 foot from the bulb. A plant 4 feet from a bulb only receives one sixteenth the light of a plant 1 foot from the bulb.

To flower well, orchids must be placed very close to the lamps. The tops of the leaves

should be 3 to 6 inches away from the bulbs. Paphiopedilums and phalaenopsis plants may be grown 6 inches from the centers of the bulbs, but should be closer if they are near the ends. Cattleyas and other light-loving plants should be within 3 inches of the centers of the bulbs. Most commercially made plant stands have adjustable shelves. If you build your own light garden, suspend the fixtures over the plants with chains so that you can adjust the distance link by link. Place small plants on inverted pots or saucers to bring their leaves up to the same level as those of the larger specimens.

Adjusting Day Length

What fluorescent lights lack in intensity, they can make up in duration. Use a timer to set the day length for your plants. The inexpensive models sold in hardware stores are fine. Some orchids require seasonal variations in day length in order to bloom. For these you will need to adjust the timer every few months to mimic the seasons. Howard Zoufaly, the American Orchid Society's most-published expert on light gardening, uses the following schedule.

November–January	16 hours/day	(spring)
February–June	18 hours/day	(summer)
July–August	16 hours/day	(fall)
September–October	12 hours/day	(winter)

Orchids under lights should be positioned to get the exposure they need. Overturned pots of various sizes can be used to lift plants with high light requirements up close to the light bulbs. In this way, species with different light demands may be grown under the same bank of lights.

Orchids Under Lights

Many orchids grow well under lights, but the most successful plants are the compact forms that can be squeezed in under the tubes so that most of their foliage is bathed in bright light. Tall, light-loving plants such as vandas and the tall dendrobiums simply won't fit under the tubes, but plants such as the phalaenopsis with short foliage and long flower spikes grow well under lights; you just have to train the spikes between and around the fixtures as they are developing. To get started try these orchids, described in the Orchid Selection Guide, beginning on page 63.

Cattleya (compact hybrids are best)
Dendrobium (compact species such as
   D. kingianum and *D. cuthbertsonii*)
Encyclia cochleata
Encyclia tampensis
Laelia (most hybrids are compact)
Laeliocattleya hybrids
Ludisia discolor
Macodes petola
Masdevallia (if conditions are cool enough)
Miltonia (species and hybrids)
Odontoglossum (multigeneric hybrids
   are best)
Oncidium (small species and hybrids)
Paphiopedilum (excellent for beginners)
Phalaenopsis (practically foolproof)
Phragmipedium
Sophronitis

As you can see, he has shifted the seasons ahead—his plants enter spring in midwinter. This schedule keeps the temperature in the growing area tolerable during the hottest part of the year, and brings spring-flowering plants into bloom for the holidays.

If your plants receive light from windows, set your timer to coincide with the sun's seasonal changes, extending the days to the lengths listed on opposite page.

When growing orchids in living areas, keep in mind that some species require a night of uninterrupted darkness for flowering. These light-sensitive species include unifoliate (single-leaved) cattleyas such as *Cattleya labiata, C. mossiae, C. percivaliana,* and *C. trianae.* Other orchids sensitive to night lighting include *Bulbophyllum falcatum, Dendrobium phalaenopsis, Oncidium splendidum,* and *Phalaenopsis amabilis.* A reading lamp left on at night produces enough light to keep these plants from blooming.

Maintaining Lights

Aside from occasionally wiping the dust off the tubes, all you have to do to keep your lights burning brightly is replace the tubes (called lamps by the manufacturers) regularly. The life of a fluorescent lamp is rated in hours. A lamp's brightness declines rapidly during the first 100 hours it burns, then decreases more slowly for the rest of its life. Don't wait until a lamp burns out to replace it—by the time it blinks out it will be burning so dimly that the plants will be suffering, even though the difference may not be noticeable to you. A lamp should be replaced after two thirds of its rated lifetime. When you install a new lamp, figure out when it will need to be replaced and write the date with a waterproof marker on the end of the tube.

Because the lamps burn so brightly at first, you will shock your plants if you replace all the lamps at once. Change the bulbs on a rotating basis. Allow a new lamp to burn for at least 100 hours before replacing another lamp in the same fixture.

GREENHOUSES

Greenhouses offer the best conditions for orchid growing—plenty of light, warm days and cool nights, lots of humidity, and space for an expanding collection. As your interest in orchids grows, there may come a day when you want a greenhouse. You will find a tremendous number of choices. Greenhouses come in many styles, shapes, and sizes, each offering its own advantages. They may be attached to the house or built as freestanding structures.

Attached Greenhouses

An attached greenhouse may be designed so that either its long side or its short side is connected to the house. If attached along the long side, it is called a lean-to greenhouse, because its sloping roof appears to lean against the house. Greenhouses attached along the short side are usually even-span greenhouses, with symmetrical peak roofs and sides. Even-span greenhouses are generally superior to lean-to greenhouses because they capture more sunlight, offer better climate control, and can be more easily expanded.

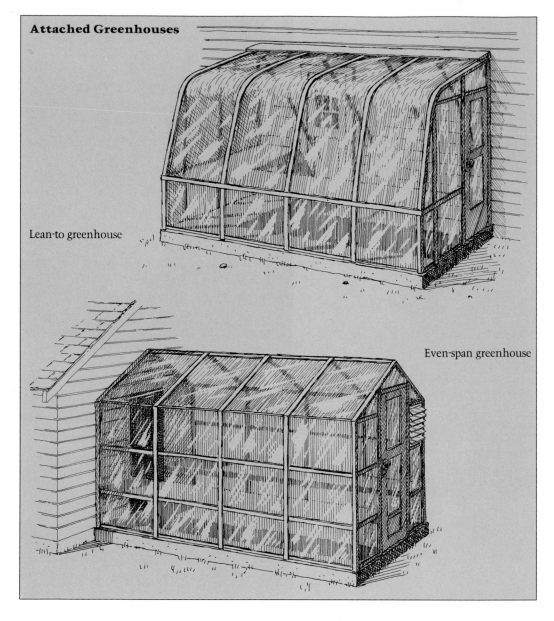

Attached Greenhouses

Lean-to greenhouse

Even-span greenhouse

Attached greenhouses with lean-to or even-span designs are relatively inexpensive and easy to build. Water and electricity can be easily brought into the greenhouse from the home systems. The solar energy they capture can be transferred to the home, especially in lean-to designs. An attached greenhouse can make a delightfully sunny living area.

Freestanding Greenhouses
Freestanding greenhouses are usually even-span designs, and are available in a variety of shapes and sizes. You can choose from a number of designs, from the traditional doghouse shape to fancy domes and gothic forms. Freestanding greenhouses are the brightest and easiest to control, but they are more expensive than attached greenhouses.

Situating a Greenhouse
Build your greenhouse where it will receive direct sunlight throughout the day. It is easy to reduce the light intensity in a greenhouse, but impossible to increase it without using artificial lights. When choosing and situating an attached greenhouse, pay particular attention to the position of the greenhouse in relation to the sun. For best results, a lean-to greenhouse should have an eastern and southern exposure. A shaded west side will reduce the chance of overheating, which is sometimes a problem in lean-to greenhouses.

Building Your Own Greenhouse
Many companies offer prefabricated greenhouse kits; you will find their advertisements in the *American Orchid Society Bulletin*

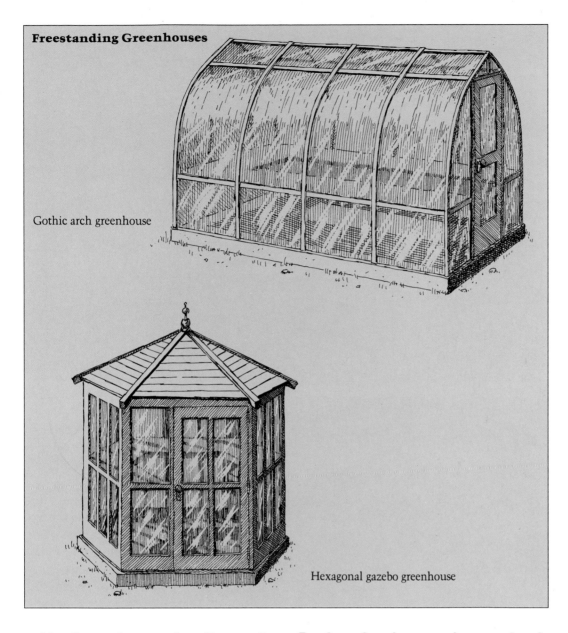

Freestanding Greenhouses

Gothic arch greenhouse

Hexagonal gazebo greenhouse

and in other garden magazines. If you prefer to start from scratch, Ortho's book *How to Build & Use Greenhouses* is one of many sources of information for the do-it-yourselfer.

Greenhouse Equipment and Supplies

In addition to the greenhouse structure, you will need benches for the plants, heating and cooling systems, and possibly a humidifier. These systems can be as simple or extravagant as you wish. The more automatic controls you install, the more time you will have to enjoy your plants. The equipment you choose will depend greatly on your climate. Find out what systems are used in your area by attending orchid society meetings and by visiting the greenhouses of other orchid growers.

Benches Greenhouse supply companies offer rot-resistant wooden benches with galvanized pipe frames. Simple, less expensive benches may be built with wooden frames or with cinderblocks and redwood boards.

Heating systems If your home has a hot-water or steam heating system, you may be able to extend the system into your greenhouse. If not, or if you have a freestanding greenhouse, you have a choice of gas, oil, and electric greenhouse heaters. Hydronic heaters, oil- or gas-fired hot-water systems, are also available. Greenhouse heaters should be thermostatically controlled to maintain those critical night temperatures accurately.

Right: Commercial greenhouses are heated and cooled by large, automatic systems. When a crop is this valuable, no expense is spared. Below: The heating and cooling systems for small, hobby greenhouses are less complicated and expensive than the ones used in sprawling commercial greenhouses. A single gas-fired heater will protect plants on frosty winter nights. Oil-fired, electric, and steam or hot-water units are also available.

Cooling and ventilation systems To keep the temperature in the greenhouse from sky-rocketing on sunny days, make sure there is adequate ventilation. Automatic vent operators make it much easier to control the temperature in a greenhouse. These units automatically open and close vents in the roof in response to changes in temperature.

In hot areas with low relative humidity, evaporative coolers set into an opening in an outside wall will economically cool and humidify the air. In an evaporative cooler, water is constantly circulated through fiber pads by a pump in a reservoir at the bottom of the unit. Air is pulled through the wet pads to cool the greenhouse in the same way that water cools your skin when you get out of a swimming pool on a breezy day. The water in the reservoir is replenished by a float valve hooked up to the plumbing. Evaporative coolers are very effective in dry areas—millions of people in the hot western and southwestern United States depend on them for relief in the summer months.

Humidifiers Two types of humidifiers are commonly used in greenhouses. Aerosol humidifiers discharge tiny droplets of water into the air. These droplets evaporate almost instantaneously, cooling the air and raising the humidity. Pad and fan type humidifiers are evaporative coolers installed inside the greenhouse. Instead of pulling in outside air, these units recirculate air within the greenhouse.

Whatever type of humidifier you choose, be sure to hook it up to the plumbing system so that you won't have to keep refilling it, and install a humidistat for automatic control. In most cases, you will want to set the controls to maintain the relative humidity at about 60 percent.

OUTDOOR GROWING AREAS

Orchids can be grown outdoors in some regions of the country. Southern Florida and Hawaii are an orchid grower's dream—many plants can simply be tied to the trees in the backyard. Californians grow cymbidiums in pots on the patio or entryway, and San Franciscans and other fog-dwellers have an ideal climate for cool-growing orchids such as odontoglossums and masdevallias. When growing orchids outdoors, keep in mind that they will be exposed to many more pests than will plants grown indoors. Snails and slugs can be particularly damaging. If you have a tree that allows dappled sunlight to penetrate its branches, you can hang your plants from the lower limbs to keep them up out of slugs' way. Otherwise build a bench to get the plants off the ground. You may need to shade an outdoor bench; lath and screen work nicely. Keep a vigilant lookout for early signs of insect infestation and treat problems as soon as you discover them.

Summering Orchids Outdoors

In areas with warm, humid summers, it is tempting to take plants outdoors for the summer. Many orchids benefit from a summer outside, but the threat of pests and diseases to which orchids grown outdoors are susceptible is compounded by the possibility that you may bring the beasts indoors with the plants in the fall. Once inside, pests can attack the orchids as they are adapting to the shock of being moved and may also infest your other houseplants. To minimize the danger, inspect your plants carefully, treat any problems you discover before you bring the plants in, and isolate them for a while after you bring them back inside to be sure they are free of pests.

Cymbidiums are pampered greenhouse plants in some parts of the country, but in the coastal regions of California, they are practically care-free patio plants.

Orchids as a Hobby

Orchid growing is one of the oldest and best organized of plant hobbies. Orchid societies and shows, mail-order catalogs, books, and periodicals are all available to the orchid lover.

Growing just one orchid, for many people, is like trying to eat just one potato chip. What may start as a casual interest in maintaining the health of an orchid received as a gift can easily develop into a delightful hobby. As you see your first plants grow and bloom, your success will encourage you to learn more about orchids and to experiment with other kinds.

If this is the case with you, you have plenty of company. Orchid societies meet regularly in metropolitan areas across the country. At these meetings professional orchid growers, avid amateurs, and enthusiastic beginners compare experiences and ideas and trade plants and tips. It's an easy and enjoyable way to learn about orchids.

As you delve into the orchid hobby you will discover many nurseries and garden-supply firms that specialize in orchids. These specialists offer a much greater selection of species and hybrids than do florists or plant shops, and the colorful, informative catalogs that some publish make delightful reading.

This chapter describes orchid societies and discusses the best ways to expand an orchid collection. A list of sources includes a selection of books and periodicals and the names and addresses of mail-order orchid companies and firms that specialize in indoor gardening supplies and greenhouses.

Orchids are challenging, fascinating, and strikingly different from other plants. In addition to evoking amazement and delight, orchids are a great source of satisfaction. There is nothing quite like the pleasure of decorating your home with unusual plants that you've grown yourself. Brassia gireoudiana, aptly called the spider orchid, fills a room with its heady fragrance and invites superlatives from admirers.

ORCHID SOCIETIES

Gardeners are great joiners. There are more than sixty plant societies in the United States alone. Such groups include the American Gourd Society, the Sempervivum Fanciers Association—and even an International Carnivorous Plant Society. But orchid societies, as you will see in the following section, are in a class of their own.

The American Orchid Society

The American Orchid Society (AOS) is one of the largest plant societies, boasting nearly 26,000 members. Its monthly magazine, the *American Orchid Society Bulletin,* is probably the main reason it has so many members. The *Bulletin* contains more than one hundred pages of articles on orchid culture, trends in orchid breeding, book reviews, questions and answers about orchids, and fascinating accounts of the discovery of new species. Most of the articles are illustrated with splendid color photographs. The advertising section is a valuable resource, listing sources of orchid plants, orchid-growing supplies, and even entire greenhouses.

In addition to the *Bulletin,* the AOS publishes *Lindleyana,* a scientific journal for the technically minded orchidist. Its articles cover developments in orchid research. Topics such as systematics, physiology, phytochemistry, cytology, anatomy and morphology, pollination biology, and evolution are all discussed in detail in this journal.

The American Orchid Society is very active in evaluating orchids by sanctioning orchid shows and sponsoring 19 regional judging centers. The results of these judgings are reported in another periodical, the *Awards Quarterly.* Published every three months by the AOS, the *Awards Quarterly* is devoted to descriptions of all the new, award-winning orchids. Some of the descriptions are illustrated with color photographs.

In addition to these three periodicals, the AOS also publishes and co-publishes a number of books on orchids and orchid-related subjects. Members of the American Orchid Society may buy these and other books from its office at a 10 percent discount.

The American Orchid Society's activities are by no means limited to the printed page. It conducts annual meetings and co-sponsors the triennial World Orchid Conferences. Its committees work internationally in the fields of education, research, conservation, and orchid history.

Membership dues for the AOS are currently $28 per year ($34 for foreign memberships). A membership includes a subscription to the *American Orchid Society Bulletin* and a copy of the *Handbook on Orchid Culture,* a yearbook, a booklist, and other benefits. See Sources, page 61, for the address and phone number of the society.

Local AOS-affiliated societies The American Orchid Society works with over 400 affiliated orchid societies throughout the United States and in 40 other countries. At the monthly meetings of these groups, guest speakers give slide programs on subjects such as orchid growing, taxonomy, conservation, and breeding. Experienced local growers share their tips and tricks. Members bringing plants for the show table assemble an inspiring and educational assortment of well-grown specimens. You will also find inexpensive plants for sale at these meetings (see Finding Bargains, page 60). Membership fees in local societies are not included in the AOS dues, but are generally very inexpensive. Contact the American Orchid Society for information on the meetings of the local group nearest you.

The Cymbidium Society of America

This group could be called the Cymbidium and Paphiopedilum Society of America, for its bimonthly publication *The Orchid Advocate* contains a wealth of information on both of these genera. Membership costs $15 a year and includes six issues of *The Orchid Advocate.* International memberships are also available; these vary from $20 to $30. Five of this society's six regional branches are in southern California; the sixth is located in New Zealand.

OBTAINING ORCHIDS

Orchids are available from many sources, but most plants are purchased in flower shops, garden centers, and orchid nurseries. Even grocery stores occasionally have flowering phalaenopsis plants and cattleyas in pots trimmed with colorful foil and confetti.

In this shop, plants are grouped by genus for easy comparison. A display of modern paphiopedilum hybrids provides an assortment of subtle variations in form and color.

Orchids From Shops

Plant nurseries and flower shops are some of the best places for the beginning orchid grower to obtain plants. The plants are always mature; in fact, they have to be in bloom for the store to carry them. Blooming plants purchased from these shops can be expensive, but you are paying for convenience and the opportunity to choose the flowers that please you.

The plants you find in grocery stores have often been subjected to some fairly trying times. The distribution system for flowers and plants varies among regions and markets, but in general orchids are grown in wholesale nurseries, from which they are shipped to smaller nurseries. These smaller nurseries distribute plants to local retailers. This means that an orchid may have been packed and shipped several times in the weeks preceding its appearance on the retailer's shelf. This torturous system works because orchids are so durable, but you still want to make sure the plant hasn't been overly stressed en route.

Look at the leaves. They should be firm and unbroken, but slight damage is no cause for worry. Inspect any visible roots—are they a healthy white with greenish tips? Lift the pot and peek in the holes in the bottom. The potting medium may be slightly decomposed, but you should still be able to make out the individual pieces. Any roots visible through the drainage holes may be dark, but they should not be slimy and rotten.

A plant with an inflorescence that is just beginning to mature is ideal. One or two of the lowest flowers will be open, but the rest should still be in bud. Look carefully at the open flowers. Are they pleasing? Except for slight variations in size and in intensity of the colors, the plant will always produce flowers like the ones you are seeing, so make sure they are what you want. The main priority, of course, is to select the flowers you like, but it doesn't hurt to consider whether they are good examples of the species or hybrid. This will become more important to you as your collection grows.

Orchids by Mail

There are hundreds of orchid nurseries in the mail-order business. The big nurseries publish glossy color catalogs filled with photographs and accurate descriptions of their plants' flowers and cultural needs. Small firms may send out only simple photocopied pages listing nothing but names and prices. The size of the business doesn't necessarily determine the quality of its plants, but until you become an expert you will need the pictures and descriptions contained in the fancy catalogs to help you make selections. See Sources (page 61) for a list of mail-order nurseries that publish informative catalogs and have a reputation for shipping high-quality plants.

Most of the large nurseries also have "plant-a-month" programs. These can be fun and a bargain to boot. The programs vary from nursery to nursery. In some cases the plants you receive are a complete surprise; in others you can specify the genus and flower colors you prefer.

Deciphering mail-order catalogs   The best orchid catalogs spell everything out for you: the plant's entire name, parentage if it is a hybrid, cultural requirements, stage of growth, plant and pot size, and of course, the price. Other catalogs are more cryptic. Their authors commonly abbreviate the genus names and may use a great deal of jargon in the descriptions. In the case of hybrids, the descriptions may not tell what the flowers actually look like, but how the breeder expects (or hopes) they will turn out. Purchasing hybrids that have never bloomed before is a game of chance. Some seedlings may mature to produce award-winning flowers, but others will be duds—at least as far as the judges are concerned. Because orchid breeders vary in their ability to produce fine hybrids consistently, you will want to consider a company's reputation before purchasing unbloomed seedlings.

Catalog writers use a number of different methods for describing plant size. Most commonly, the size of the pot is listed. (Pots are measured across the rim.) This gives you a general indication of the size of the plant, but it doesn't tell the whole story. To complete the picture, good catalogs will include additional information to indicate what the plants are like in each pot size. "Blooming size" generally means the plant will bloom within a year of purchase, given proper care. For cattleyas and other sympodial orchids, many growers list the number of pseudobulbs. Monopodial orchids are commonly sold by the inch. Phalaenopsis plants, for example, are measured from the tip of one leaf to the tip of the opposite leaf.

If you are just starting out, limit your purchases to mature, blooming-size plants. These usually come in pots 4 inches across or larger. Later, when you have more experience, you might want to try growing the less expensive immature plants shipped in community pots (shallow trays containing between one and three dozen seedlings) or in small individual containers.

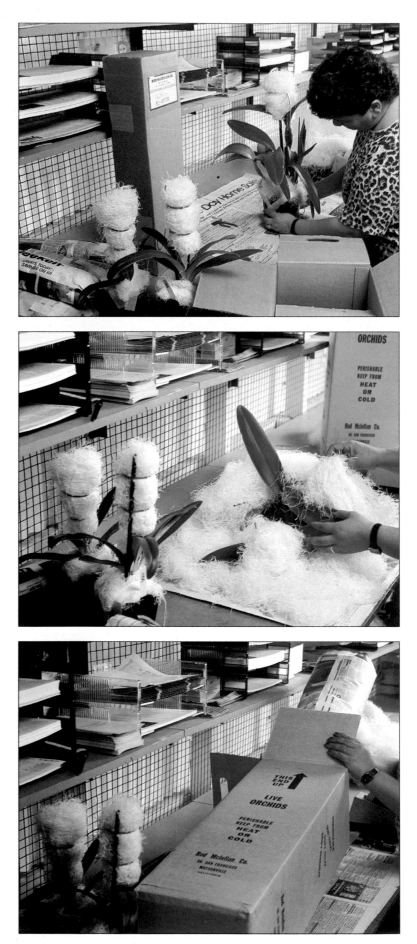

Endangered Orchids

The orchid's popularity has had some unfortunate effects. When the Victorians discovered the beauty of these plants, a huge demand was created. At that time, of course, there weren't any wholesale orchid nurseries with modern propagation facilities; plants had to be collected from the wild. Orchid sellers sponsored plant hunters on expeditions throughout the world. These plant hunters were very good—too good—at their jobs, sending back shipments weighing tons and containing thousands of plants. When one of these botanical conquistadors found a valuable species, he took every plant he could find, wreaking ecological havoc. Most plants were scoured from the wild only to be killed by the well-meaning but misinformed hobbyists who purchased them. Some species became extinct. Although the number of orchids removed from the wilds for collectors has diminished since the Victorian orchid boom, you will still find collected orchids for sale. If commercial collection continues, more species may become extinct.

Another, much greater danger to wild orchids is the destruction of their habitats. When a tropical forest is cleared, the orchids are destroyed—permanently. Unlike collection, habitat destruction removes all the orchids, not just the pretty ones valued by hobbyists. Experts estimate that over 200 billion orchid plants are destroyed by land-clearing operations each year.

What can be done? You can discourage the gathering of wild orchids by limiting your purchases to plants propagated in orchid nurseries. In addition to being ecologically sound, orchids from nurseries grow more vigorously and usually have better flowers than those of collected specimens. If you must buy a wild plant, ask to see proof that it has been legally imported, but keep in mind that legal restrictions usually fall short of adequate protection for the species.

Habitat destruction is a more difficult subject; the land is often cleared to grow food for people to eat. Organizations such as The Nature Conservancy and the World Wildlife Fund are involved in protecting wild plants and plant habitats. If you are interested in finding out about the activities of these groups, write to them at the following addresses:

The Nature Conservancy
1800 North Kent Street
Arlington, VA 22209
703-841-5300

World Wildlife Fund
and the Conservation Foundation
1250 Twenty-fourth Street NW
Suite 500
Washington, DC 20037
202-293-4800

Opposite: Mail-order orchids are routinely shipped across the country and around the world. The plants may be shipped in all stages of growth, from tiny plantlet to mature specimen. When an orchid is sent in bud (with unopened flowers), the flower stalk is secured to a stake and carefully padded. Then the rest of the plant is wrapped in packing material and eased into a carton. Orchids handled in this way reach their destinations healthy, unbroken, and ready to burst into bloom.

Bulldozers clear a tropical forest in Brazil.

Small orchid nurseries usually don't have space for a separate shop. At this nursery, the plants that are for sale are placed on a bench along the side of the greenhouse. The adjacent bench contains parent plants for a breeding program. This informal atmosphere adds to the charm of the orchid hobby.

Caring for new arrivals Orchids may be shipped in pots or bare root, depending on the preference of the customer and the practice of the grower. Many people order bare-root plants to minimize the shipping costs and to allow them to pot the plants in their own mediums and containers.

When you receive a bare-root plant, inspect the leaves and roots, cutting off any damaged portions with a sharp, sterile knife. Then pot it and treat it as you would any other newly potted plant (see page 32).

Potted orchids are allowed to dry out before they are packed so that they won't rot in the box. When you receive a potted orchid, inspect the leaves and cut off any damaged parts with a sharp sterile knife. Then water the plant. If the pot arrives broken, slip the rootball into a new pot. Unless the roots are badly damaged, you don't need to disturb them.

The people at mail-order nurseries watch the weather carefully, timing their shipments to coincide with mild weather. If you live in a cold climate, however, you may not be able to obtain mail-order orchids at all during the winter. Plants damaged by cold generally turn black a few days after arrival.

Most mail-order nurseries guarantee their plants. If you receive plants that are badly damaged by rough handling or temperature extremes, get in touch with the nursery. The plant will be replaced or you will be asked to file a claim with the carrier.

Finding Bargains

If you are looking for bargains, join an orchid society. At orchid society meetings, plants are exchanged in a spirit of appreciation and enjoyment; profit is rarely considered. At these meetings you might find local growers selling plants for very low prices, as well as a raffle table of plants you might win for a dollar or two. On a less formal basis, society members increase the variety of their collections by trading divisions, seedlings, and keikis.

Orchid shows can also be a good source of plants. Although the exquisite specimens in the display area will not be for sale, most shows have areas where growers offer plants for sale at reasonable prices. Usually the best bargains at these shows are bare-root orchids or recently potted divisions. Toward the end of the show the sellers may reduce the prices on their remaining plants to avoid having to carry them home.

Orchid nurseries also have sales, usually toward the end of the blooming season when the plants have few remaining blooms.

SOURCES

This section provides listings of firms in the orchid and orchid-supply business, the addresses of orchid societies, and recommended books and periodicals on orchids. The address of a virus testing service is also included.

Orchids and Supplies

The following listing includes some of the largest mail-order suppliers of orchids and orchid supplies such as pots, mediums, and fertilizers. All of these firms publish illustrated catalogs with informative descriptions of the plants, and most of the catalogs contain color photographs. Hundreds of other mail-order firms sell orchids. Look for their advertisements in the *American Orchid Society Bulletin* and in the periodicals published by other orchid societies. An impressively complete list of mail-order orchid firms may be found in *Gardening by Mail* by Barbara Barton. It is available in bookstores or from Tusker Press, Box 597004, San Francisco, CA 94159; 415-931-7877.

Fennell's Orchid Jungle
26715 Southwest 157th Avenue
Homestead, FL 33031
800-327-2832

J & L Orchids
20 Sherwood Road
Easton, CT 06612
203-261-3772
(orchid plants only)

Jones and Scully
18955 Southwest 168th Street
Miami, FL 33187
305-238-7000

Kensington Orchids, Inc.
3301 Plyers Mill Road
Kensington, MD 20895
301-933-0036

Rod McLellan Company
1450 El Camino Real
South San Francisco, CA 94080
415-871-5655

Orchids by Hausermann, Inc.
2N 134 Addison Road
Villa Park, IL 60181
312-543-6855

Stewart Orchids
3376 Foothill Road
Box 550
Carpinteria, CA 93013
805-684-5448

The Orchid Ranch
1330 Isabel Avenue
Livermore, CA 94550
415-447-7171

Yamamoto Dendrobiums
Box 235
Mountain View, HI 96771
808-968-6955

Societies

These are the addresses of the orchid societies described on page 56.

American Orchid Society, Inc.
6000 South Olive Avenue
West Palm Beach, FL 33405
407-585-8666

Cymbidium Society of America, Inc.
Membership Secretary:
Jo Johnston
6881 Wheeler Avenue
Westminster, CA 92683
714-894-5421

Books

The orchid selection guide in this book presents an overview of some of the most popular orchids. For descriptions of the thousands of other species found in cultivation, refer to the books in the following list. The authors of most of these books use botanical language, but *Home Orchid Growing* by Rebecca Northen is written for nonprofessionals. Many of these books are available at a discount through the American Orchid Society. Write to them for a free copy of their current book list.

Encyclopaedia of Cultivated Orchids
Alex D. Hawkes
Boston: Faber and Faber, 1965
602 pages, $75.

Home Orchid Growing, Third Edition
Rebecca Tyson Northen
New York: Van Nostrand Reinhold, 1970
374 pages, $40.

Manual of Cultivated Orchid Species, Revised Edition
Helmut Bechtel, Phillip Cribb, and Edmund Launert.
Cambridge: MIT Press, 1986
444 pages, $75.

Orchid Genera Illustrated
Tom Sheehan and Marion Sheehan
Ithaca: Cornell University Press, 1985
208 pages, $14.95 (soft cover)

Periodicals

Most of the magazines listed below are published by, or in association with, an orchid society. See page 56 for more information about the publications of the American Orchid Society and the Cymbidium Society of America.

American Orchid Society Bulletin
Published monthly by the American Orchid Society

Awards Quarterly
Published quarterly by the American Orchid Society

Lindleyana
Published quarterly by the American Orchid Society

The Orchid Advocate
Published bimonthly by the Cymbidium Society of America

The Orchid Digest
Published quarterly by the Orchid Digest Corporation
Membership Secretary:
Mrs. Norman H. Atkinson
Box 916
Carmichael, CA 95609

Lights and Garden Equipment

This is a partial list of firms that specialize in lights and other indoor gardening equipment:

Applied Hydroponics, Inc.
3135 Kerner Blvd.
San Rafael, CA 94901
415-459-7898

Environmental Concepts
710 Northwest 57th Street
Fort Lauderdale, FL 33309
305-491-4490
(offers light and other meters)

Indoor Gardening Supplies
Box 40567
Detroit, MI 48240
313-427-6160

Verilux, Inc.
Box 1512
Greenwich, CT 06836
203-869-3750

R. D. & Associates
Box 1616
Pomona, CA 91768
(manufactures RD20® bactericide)

Prefabricated Greenhouses

For more information on home greenhouses, see Ortho's book *How to Build & Use Greenhouses*. For additional information on greenhouse suppliers, see the *American Orchid Society Bulletin*.

Gothic Arch Greenhouses
Box 1564
Mobile, AL 36633
205-432-7529

Lord & Burnham
Box 255
Irvington, NY 10533
914-591-8800

Virus Testing Services

If you suspect that one of your plants is infected with a virus, this company will test a leaf sample for you.

Orchis Laboratories
86F Mason Road
Burdett, NY 14818
607-277-0424

Orchid Selection Guide

This gallery of photographs and plant descriptions includes instructions for growing the orchids best suited for windowsills, light gardens, or greenhouses.

Most of the plants mentioned in this guide are recommended for beginning orchid growers who want beautiful plants that will bloom in their homes. But this does not mean that all of these orchids will grow under the same conditions. Homes vary a great deal in light intensity, temperature, and humidity. Growing areas vary from tiny kitchen windowsills to spacious sun porches. Some of the species in this guide don't grow well indoors, but are popular patio plants in mild regions of the United States. Other species do well indoors under lights. The key to success with orchids is simple: choose plants that have cultural requirements you can easily meet.

The entries in this guide are organized alphabetically by genus. Most genera contain many more species than could possibly be included here. Occasionally, as in the case of *Cattleya labiata,* the species is hardly ever grown any more, but its hybrid progeny are found in collections all over the world. These horticulturally important species are included to give an overall impression of the hybrids.

In the world of orchids, hybrids are extremely important. Most of the orchids offered for sale are hybrids. Every year new hybrids are introduced, most differing from their predecessors only in nuances of color and form. The last part of each genus description highlights the most recent work of the orchid breeders.

When selecting orchids, it is best to choose plants with a particular spot in mind. The morning light that enters this window meets the energy needs of cattleya hybrids and a miniature cymbidium without burning the leaves. Within a growing area, position plants with the highest light requirements closest to the glass. Plants with sensitive foliage should be placed toward the front of the group where they will be partially shaded by the others.

WHAT KIND OF ORCHID IS THAT?

Orchids are named under the same international system that governs the naming of all other plants. But the orchid family is incredibly large and orchid species interbreed so easily that it is sometimes difficult to tell where one species stops and the next begins. Nevertheless, taxonomists must try to organize the myriad forms and colors of orchids into neat—and discrete—categories.

The complexity of these categories is reflected in the fine distinctions made among apparently similar plants and hybrids that have elaborate family trees. However, the basic principles are those followed in the naming of any plant. Few people can rattle off the various rules and exceptions of orchid naming, but for any hobbyist, even a general notion of the system will contribute to the enjoyment to be derived from this remarkably diverse family of plants.

HOW ORCHIDS ARE NAMED

To understand how an orchid gets its name, it is best to start at the top, with the orchid family. For most plants the next major category used below family is the genus (or genera if you are speaking of more than one). Because the orchid family is so large, botanists use intermediate categories between the family and genus called tribe and subtribe, categories that are helpful because they show how the plants in the different genera are related.

The genus *Miltonia*, for example, is in the subtribe Oncidiinae. This subtribe also includes the genera *Oncidium, Odontoglossum,* and *Brassia,* all of which have similar characteristics and hybridize easily. A family tree makes it easier to see how these groups are related:

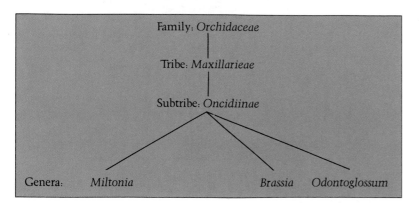

The genus name, such as *Miltonia* or *Brassia,* is an essential part of an orchid's identification. To show that it is a genus name, the word is printed in italics and the first letter is capitalized. All of the plants in this guide are listed alphabetically by their genus names.

A genus is divided into species, the basic units of classification in both the plant and animal kingdoms. Species names are printed in italics but are not capitalized. The genus *Miltonia,* for example, contains the species *spectabilis.* An easy way to remember how genus and species names are related is to look at the first few letters of both words. Genus is *gen*eral; species is *speci*fic. The plants in a given species are all quite similar, but you will still find differences in flower size, shape, and color, as well as small differences in the leaves, stems, and pseudobulbs.

Sometimes certain plants in a species share a characteristic that makes them different from others in the species, but not quite different enough to justify giving them a new species name. If such a group is found in nature, it is called a variety. Variety names are preceded by the abbreviation var. and are printed in lowercase italics. *Miltonia spectabilis* var. *moreliana,* for example, has rose rather than white flower petals, but aside from this difference in color it is virtually identical to the white-petaled forms of *Miltonia spectabilis.* If these plants were put on a family tree, the tree would look like this:

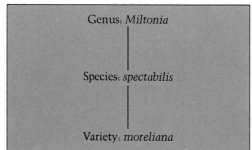

Variety names are used primarily by botanists, who study populations of wild plants. In horticulture, the study of cultivated plants, the term cultivar (from *culti*vated *var*iety) is used more frequently. Cultivars are plants selected for their desirable features and propagated in ways that perpetuate those features. A cultivar may be selected from a species, a hybrid, or a variety. It may be propagated by division, offshoots, mericloning, or by any other method that produces offspring similar to the parent. Cultivar names are printed in roman letters. The first letter is capitalized, and the name is enclosed in single quotes.

For example, it turns out that one of the prettiest forms of *Miltonia spectabilis* var. *moreliana* has been widely cultivated and awarded. This clone, named 'Royalty', is a cultivar of a variety. It takes its place at the bottom of the family tree:

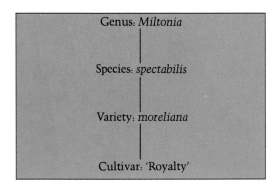

Genus: *Miltonia*

Species: *spectabilis*

Variety: *moreliana*

Cultivar: 'Royalty'

Orchids With More Than One Name

Unfortunately, everyone doesn't always use the same names for orchids. Over the years, plant taxonomists have tried and discarded several schemes for organizing orchids along evolutionary lines, and things still haven't settled down completely. The goal—a classification system that shows how plants are related—is worthwhile, but becomes difficult to attain when many names must be changed to reflect a new botanical discovery. Placing communication before evolutionary accuracy, many books and catalogs list orchids under the names by which they are most commonly known, sometimes ignoring the latest rulings of the plant taxonomists. In this book, we use the names deemed to be botanically correct at the time of publication. If an orchid is widely known by another name (usually a former name), this name is listed in parentheses.

Hybrids

The fuzzy lines that separate the different kinds of orchids may cause headaches for taxonomists, but one person's bane is another's boon: the orchid's wide-ranging sexual compatibility gives orchid breeders the artistic freedom to produce stunning new orchids

by crossing plants that are only remotely related. The offspring of these crosses are called hybrids, and they are named by an odd and often confusing system.

When two orchid species in the same genus are crossed, the resulting hybrid seedlings are given a name. Orchid breeders name their hybrids after family members, spouses, mountains, rivers—almost anything goes these days as long as it doesn't sound like Latin. (Many old hybrid names sounded like Latin, but in 1959 the taxonomists changed the rules to prohibit Latinized hybrid names because it was difficult to tell the species from the hybrids.) To be made official, a hybrid name must be registered with the Royal Horticultural Society (RHS), which lists it in *Sander's Complete List of Orchid Hybrids*. Once a hybrid has an official name, all plants resulting from a cross between those parents carry that name, even if subsequent crosses produce very different-looking results.

To return to the family tree, the name of the cross between *Miltonia spectabilis* and *Miltonia clowesii* is *Miltonia* Bluntii. You

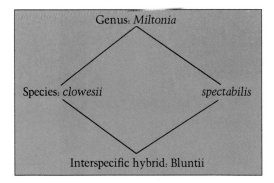

Genus: *Miltonia*

Species: *clowesii*   *spectabilis*

Interspecific hybrid: Bluntii

can tell from the word's Latin ending that this is an old hybrid, named before the rules prohibited Latinized hybrid names. *Miltonia* Bluntii is a primary hybrid, produced when a species is crossed with another species. Primary hybrids are not as common in cultivation as more complex hybrids, which are produced when a hybrid is crossed with a species or with another hybrid. For many years, orchid fashion dictated that flowers be extremely large and brightly colored, characteristics produced through a great deal of genetic shuffling. Now that the value of species orchids is becoming more widely recognized (see Endangered Orchids, page 59), primary hybrids are coming back into vogue.

Intergeneric Hybrids

Orchid breeders have great fun crossing orchids of different genera, producing plants that can only be considered members of a new genus. This is remarkable genetics; few plants other than orchids will interbreed this way.

An intergeneric hybrid may be named in one of two ways. In the simplest way, the hybrid name is formed by combining the two genus names, as in *Miltassia* from *Miltonia* and *Brassia*. These names make it easy to remember the parents of the hybrid. The hybrid of *Miltonia spectabilis* and *Brassia verrucosa,* for example, is called *Miltassia* Charles M. Fitch. It has a popular cultivar, 'Dark Monarch'. Here is how these plants are related:

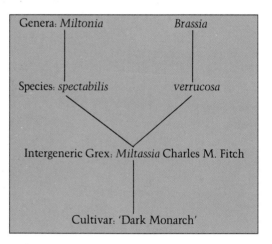

When a bigeneric hybrid (a hybrid of two genera) is crossed with a plant in yet another genus, the three names may be lumped together as in *Sophrolaeliocattleya,* the name of the cross of *Sophronitis, Laelia,* and *Cattleya.* When the names of the genera don't flow together so smoothly, taxonomists avoid making tongue twisters by giving the hybrid an entirely new name ending with the letters *ara.* For example, the hybrid *Cochlioda* × *Miltonia* × *Odontoglossum* was named *Vuylstekeara* to honor C. Vuylsteke, a Belgian orchid breeder. Another delightful hybrid, *Potinara,* results from crossing four genera: *Brassavola, Laelia, Cattleya,* and *Sophronitis.*

Putting It All Together

Believe it or not, these different aspects of orchid naming fit nicely, though with some complexity, into a single logical system. The entire family tree shows how the previous examples are related. It is often helpful, when confronted by mystifying orchid names, to try to sort them out by visualizing their place on a similar diagram.

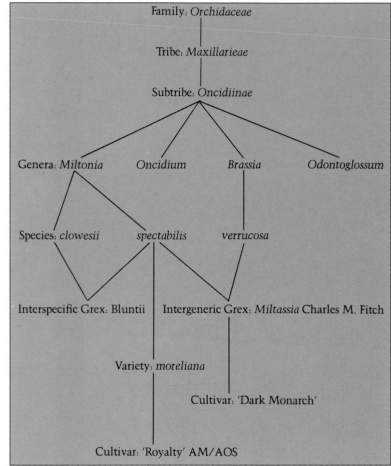

Common Names

Common orchid names are just as confusing and misleading as the common names of other plants. Although sometimes easier to pronounce, the words rarely point directly to a specific plant, and are thus of little value. A single common name often applies to several different species, species that have nothing—besides a common name—in common. For example, there seems to be at least one spider orchid on every continent, and new ones are probably dubbed every day. Better simply to call them all orchids, a very general but at least correct common name.

Most orchid species don't even have common names. The genus name is used informally as a common name. In this book, for example, when the genus *Cattleya* is discussed, the word is treated as a common name, as in "cattleyas are easy to grow."

The proud grower of this outstanding specimen Paphiopedilum chamberlainianum *'Magnifico' was awarded a Certificate of Cultural Merit (83 points) from the American Orchid Society.*

THE AWARDS OF THE AMERICAN ORCHID SOCIETY

With so many species, varieties, hybrids, and cultivars around, it is necessary to distinguish outstanding orchids from those that are merely pretty. The international awards system established by the American Orchid Society in 1945 sets standards for evaluating orchid hybrids, species selections, and individual specimen plants. The awards provide a yardstick by which the quality of new hybrids or selections may be measured and growers commended for especially well grown plants.

When evaluating an orchid, judges compare it with all others of the same type that they may have seen, not just with the other orchids in the show. In order to make such comparisons, an orchid judge goes through at least six years of training—three years as a student judge and three years on probation.

Only after this intensive training can a person become an accredited AOS judge.

Criteria for Judging Orchids

In most cases, orchids are judged solely on the basis of their flowers. The characteristics judges look for in the flowers depend to some extent on what kind of plant it is, but the flowers' color, size, shape, and substance (thickness) are always considered, as is the way in which the flowers are borne on the stems. The sharpness and clarity of any stripes, spots, or other markings on the petals are also evaluated.

The flowers of hybrids and species selections are evaluated on a 100-point scale. In order to be considered for an award, an orchid must pass an initial screening. If the judges feel the orchid has a chance of receiving an award, it is then entered in the formal judging. The best award an orchid can receive is the First Class Certificate (FCC/AOS). For this certificate, the orchid must be awarded 90 points or more. Few flowers are ever so perfect.

The Award of Merit (AM/AOS) is the next-best award, and is by no means easy to attain. For an Award of Merit, the plant must receive between 80 and 89 points. A plant bearing the letters AM/AOS after its name will have exceptionally beautiful flowers.

The third award is the Highly Commended Certificate (HCC/AOS). An HCC/AOS plant, having received between 75 and 79 points, is still an excellent orchid.

Species orchids may be eligible for two additional awards. The Certificate of Botanical Recognition (CBR/AOS) is awarded to cultivars of species or natural hybrids deemed worthy of recognition for their rarity, novelty, or educational value. The Certificate of Horticultural Merit (CHM/AOS) is given to well-grown species that are considered particularly interesting from a horticultural standpoint.

And finally, you don't have to breed a new hybrid or collect a new species to receive an AOS award. The Certificate of Cultural Merit (CCM/AOS) is awarded to outstanding specimen plants that have enjoyed perfect growing conditions. For this category, the whole plant is judged, not just the flowers. To have your efforts rewarded with a CCM/AOS is a notable achievement.

Rhyncholaelia digbyana 'Dragonstone', HCC/AOS

Brassavola David Sander

Brassavola

(bra-*sah*-vo-la)

Sympodial

Light   Medium to high

Temperature   Warm to intermediate

Flowering   Summer to fall

Care   Easy

The genus *Brassavola* is composed of Latin American epiphytes, closely related to plants in the genera *Cattleya* and *Laelia*. Their star-shaped flowers are deliciously fragrant at night, but the scent becomes almost imperceptible shortly after daybreak. Easily grown with cattleyas, brassavolas demand plenty of light but tolerate humidity as low as 40 percent. Propagate plants by dividing the growths after flowering.

Species

Rhyncholaelia digbyana (*Brassavola digbyana*) Although *Brassavola digbyana* is often used, the correct name for this species is *Rhyncholaelia digbyana*. A popular parent in crosses with cattleya and laelia, *R. digbyana* gives the large

flower size and fimbriated (fringed) lip to many cattleya hybrids. It is also worth growing in its own right for its 4- to 6-inch greenish white flowers with lacy labella and lemony fragrance. The narrow, silvery leaves are succulent and between 8 and 10 inches long. Respect its rest period; water lightly and withhold fertilizer for several months after flowering. Native from Mexico to Guatemala.

B. nodosa   This orchid is called the "lady of the night" in Latin America for its exquisite evening perfume. The 3-inch flowers may be white with tiny purple dots on the lip, greenish white, or cream. The foliage is upright, and varies in height from a compact 4 inches up to 12 inches in larger forms. Unlike *B. digbyana, B. nodosa* does not need a rest period—it usually grows and flowers throughout the year. It is native from Mexico through Central America to Peru and Venezuela; also found in the West Indies.

Hybrids

Brassavola David Sander, an early hybrid of *B. digbyana* and *B. cucullata,* has narrow, pinkish white petals and a perfectly fringed lip. Its narrow, shiny leaves are about the size of a pencil.

Brassavolas are crossed with cattleyas to form brassocattleyas, or with cattleyas and laelias to form brassolaeliocattleyas. These are described with the other cattleya hybrids, on page 70.

Brassia

(*brass*-ee-ah)

Sympodial

Light   Medium

Temperature   Intermediate

Flowering   Late spring to early summer

Care   Easy

Orchids of the genus *Brassia* are among the many orchids commonly called spider orchids. In this case the name is very descriptive. The slender, pointed sepals and petals of the flowers resemble spider legs, and the lip is shaped much like a spider's

body. Fortunately, spiders don't grow as large as these gargantuan flowers. The blossoms of some forms stretch more than 16 inches from top to bottom.

Brassias don't come in a wide variety of colors, but their hues are very appealing. Most are gold to green, speckled or banded with brown, purple, or maroon. Almost all of the 30 species have fragrant flowers. Well-grown plants may bear hundreds of blossoms, perfectly spaced on gently arching spikes. Each large, flattened pseudobulb bears two or three long leathery leaves. Most plants grow to about 2 feet tall, though some may reach 3 feet.

Brassias can be treated like cattleyas, but they should not be allowed to dry out completely when they are actively growing. Propagate them by dividing the pseudobulbs after flowering.

Species

Brassia gireoudiana The large, flattened pseudobulbs and leathery leaves of

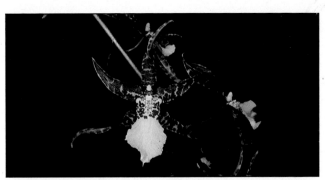

Brassidium Zanzibar Princess 'Anne', HCC/AOS

Cattleya aurantiaca 'Sally', CCM/AOS

Brassia Edvah Loo 'Mark Daniel', HCC/AOS

this species are typical of the genus. The flowers are very fragrant and measure up to 12 inches from top to bottom. The sepals and petals are greenish yellow, blotched near their bases with shiny black or brown markings. The large, pale yellow lip spreads wide at the tip. It has a few brown spots near the center. The exceptionally large, well-shaped flowers of *Brs. gireoudiana* 'Town Hill' earned it an AM/AOS. *Brs. gireoudiana* flowers in late spring to summer. It is native to Costa Rica and Panama.

Brs. maculata Very similar to *Brs. gireoudiana*, except that the flowers of this species are smaller (from 5 to 8 inches long) and are spotted with purple. They also last an exceptionally long time, up to one and a half months. The cultivar *Brs. maculata* 'Monte Vista' received an HCC/AOS. *Brs. maculata* blooms at any time between fall and spring and sometimes blooms twice a year. It is found in Guatemala, Honduras, Venezuela, Cuba, and Jamaica.

Hybrids

Crosses between *Brassia* species have produced vigorous, adaptable hybrids such as Edvah Loo *(Brs. longissima × Brs. gireoudiana)* and Rex *(Brs. gireoudiana × Brs. verrucosa)*. Both hybrids have large fragrant flowers with brown markings.

Orchid breeders often "add a little brassia" to other genera to increase flower size and plant vigor. Crosses of brassias with oncidiums produce brassidiums, a new genus of plants with large numbers of big yellow flowers variously marked with brown.

Miltonias are crossed with brassias to form miltassias, star-shaped flowers with ruffled lips. Miltassias are particularly easy to grow, flowering and growing vigorously in a wide range of temperatures.

Combinations of three genera: *Brassia, Oncidium,* and *Miltonia* result in the *Aliceara* hybrids. These plants bear dozens of enormous flowers in combinations of rich gold and maroon, yellow and chocolate, orange and yellow, and green and white.

Cattleya

(*kat*-lee-a)

Sympodial

Light Medium to high

Temperature Intermediate to warm

Flowering Variable

Care Easy

When most people think of an orchid, they think of a cattleya, the prom night corsage. Important in orchid history, the genus was named after William Cattley, the English horticulturist who first brought these beautiful plants into flower outside of their native habitat. Actually, Mr. Cattley didn't intend to discover a genus of highly evolved flowering plants; he was devoting his horticultural efforts to the lowly mosses and lichens shipped to him from South America by a plant explorer named Swainson. In preparing his shipments, Swainson used the cattleya plant's stiff leathery leaves and pseudobulbs to reinforce the bundles of mosses. Cattley's curiosity was piqued by the odd plants, so he potted them up to see what they would

do. Needless to say, they did a great deal. When the plants started blooming in 1824, Cattley showed them to John Lindley, one of England's most famous botanists. Lindley recognized that these gorgeous flowers were new to science, and named the genus *Cattleya* after its discoverer and the species *labiata,* in reference to the flower's impressive lip. Word of the discovery spread quickly, inciting an orchid mania among wealthy flower fanciers. To this day, the cattleya reigns as queen of the orchids.

Cattleyas are divided into two groups according to the number of leaves arising from the pseudobulbs. Unifoliate cattleyas have a single leaf on each pseudobulb, and grow between 1½ and 2 feet tall. The flowers, borne one to five per stem, are between 2 and 7 inches across. Hybrid flowers may be even larger. The large ruffled lip is often marked with colorful patterns. Unifoliates may also be called labiates in reference to *Cattleya labiata,* the most important species in the group. Although other unifoliates were

Cattleya bicolor 'Orchidglade', AM/AOS

Cattleya skinneri 'Many', CCM/AOS

once commonly grown, they are now expensive and difficult to obtain, having been largely supplanted by hybrids.

The species in the other group of cattleyas, the bifoliates, have two (or occasionally three) leaves atop long, slender pseudobulbs. Bifoliates range from 15 inches to 5 feet tall. The flowers, generally thicker and smaller than those of the unifoliates, are borne 10 to 25 per spike and usually last longer than those of the unifoliates.

Cattleyas are among the easiest orchids to grow. Their thick pseudobulbs enable them to withstand periods of drought, forgiving the forgetful gardener. Very attentive gardeners may need to be careful not to overwater. The growing medium should dry out almost completely between waterings. (See page 22 for tips on how to check the moisture content of the growing medium.) Plants growing in fir bark generally need to be watered about once a week when in active growth. After flowering they enter a resting phase lasting a month or two. In-

crease the intervals between waterings and don't fertilize at all during this period.

Cattleya flowers last about two weeks on the plant. Cut flowers last about a week. To make them last as long as possible, don't cut the flowers until they have fully expanded and thickened—about three to five days after they open. Although they may be richly fragrant on the plant, the flowers lose their fragrance when cut.

Species

Species cattleyas have largely given way to hybrids, but some superior species forms are still available.

Cattleya aurantiaca This bifoliate grows to about 1½ feet tall. The flowers are thick, fragrant, bright orange or orange-red, and about 1½ inches across. It blooms from summer to fall. Commonly used in breeding, *C. aurantiaca* is an ancestor of many of the orange to red hybrids. It occurs in Mexico, Guatemala, El Salvador, Honduras, and Nicaragua.

C. bicolor A tall species, the shoots of this bifoliate

may reach 4 feet. Its flowers are very fragrant, and spread up to 4 inches across. The sepals and petals are golden green with a coppery tinge, and the narrow lip is a brilliant purplish red. The plant flowers in the fall and may bloom again in spring. It is found in Brazil.

C. guttata Usually about 3 feet tall, vigorous forms of this bifoliate may grow to 5 feet. The fragrant yellow-green flowers are variously marked with purple. The lip is usually magenta, and may have white lobes. It flowers from late fall to winter. *C. guttata* is often used in hybridization. It is native to Brazil.

C. labiata This long-popular unifoliate grows up to 2 feet tall. Its rosy flowers have excellent proportions and a fine texture. The large, ruffled lip for which the species is named is deep rose with dark lines leading to a pair of yellow spots in the throat. In addition to being beautiful, the flowers are fragrant and long lasting. The plants bloom in fall in response to the shorten-

ing days. A lamp left on in the evening during the fall months can prevent flowering. It is native to Brazil.

C. skinneri This is a relatively short bifoliate, only reaching about 2 feet tall. Its rose, purple, or white flowers are about 3 inches across. They have a delightful glittery texture and sometimes a faint fragrance. The plant has an excellent habit and makes many new growths every year under good growing conditions. It flowers from late winter to spring. Native to a large area, this species may be found in Mexico, Guatemala, Honduras, Costa Rica, Colombia, Venezuela, and Bolivia.

Hybrids

Thousands of cattleya hybrids have been produced, many involving *C. labiata*. Some are crosses within the *Cattleya* genus, but most involve crosses with plants in other genera. The following are the most common of these intergeneric hybrids.

Brassolaeliocattleya (Brassavola × Laelia × Cattleya)

Brassolaeliocattleya Clyde's Melody 'Orchidglade', AM/AOS

Cymbidium Bulbarrow 'Pinkie', HCC/AOS

Epicattleya (Epidendrum × Cattleya)
Laeliocattleya (Laelia × Cattleya)
Potinara (Brassavola × Cattleya × Laelia × Sophronitis)
Sophrolaeliocattleya (Sophronitis × Laelia × Cattleya)

The range of colors, patterns, and fragrances found in these hybrids is astounding. Flowers in the orchid tones (rose, pink, and lavender) may have lips of vivid chartreuse, with yellow markings in the throat. Yellow flowers may be pure gold or tinged with green and often have red markings on the lip. Green forms with yellow- or red-marked lips often have wonderful lemony fragrances. Whites and semialbas usually have lips marked with red, purple, or yellow. Sizzling reds and pastels provide exotic splashes of color.

Multicolored flowers, flowers with splashes and spots, flowers large and small—it is no wonder that some orchid fanciers devote their entire collections to cattleyas and cattleya hybrids.

Cymbidium

(sim-*bid*-ee-um)

Sympodial

Light Standards: bright; miniatures: medium to bright

Temperature Standards: cool; miniatures: cool to intermediate

Flowering Variable; peak in early spring

Care Average

Substantial, long-lasting cymbidium flowers are as common in flower shops as cattleya flowers. The cymbidium's flower colors, which include all but the blue part of the rainbow, are often combined in lovely patterns. Imagine, for example, a pistachio green flower with a scarlet and white lip. The individual flowers are popular for corsages and when left on the plant last between 8 and 10 weeks.

Hardly anyone grows species cymbidiums anymore. Years of intense breeding have given us hybrids that outshine the species in flower form, color, and longevity. They are also easier to grow, tolerating broader ranges of temperature and blooming more freely.

Cymbidium hybrids fall into two main groups, standards and miniatures. Standard cymbidiums bear flowers between 3 and 5 inches across and grow up to 3 feet tall. They require bright sunlight and very cool night temperatures. Along the California coast, where these requirements are easily satisfied, standard cymbidiums are considered low-maintenance outdoor plants. In other areas, standard cymbidiums are rather difficult cool-greenhouse plants.

The flowers of miniature cymbidiums are between 1 and 3 inches in diameter. Although they are still too large to be considered true miniature orchids (which are generally less than 1 foot tall), their 1- to 2-foot maximum height makes them more manageable. Although many miniatures will produce flowers in warmer temperatures than will standards, their high light requirement still makes them greenhouse or outdoor plants.

Standards and miniatures are semiterrestrial plants. They need to be kept moist at all times, and are potted in plastic pots in mixes that retain large quantities of water while still allowing adequate aeration. As with other orchids, many mixes are suitable. Some growers use fine fir bark; others pot their cymbidiums in a mixture of 20 percent peat moss, 45 percent medium-grade fir bark, and 35 percent redwood chips. Commercial mixes are also available.

Standard Hybrids

Most standard hybrids are produced for the cut-flower trade, where timing is critical. As a result, you can choose plants for bloom in three different seasons. Early hybrids flower before Christmas, midseason hybrids bloom from January to April, and late-season hybrids bloom from April to May. Award-winning hybrids are available in all blooming-season categories.

Miniature Hybrids

Miniatures bloom at any time from late fall to spring. A variety of colors is available.

Dendrobium aggregatum 'M.G.R.', CCM/AOS

Dendrobium chrysotoxum 'Fred Fuchs, Jr.', HCC/AOS

Dendrobium johnsoniae 'Mission Bay', HCC/AOS

Dendrobium

(den-*droh*-bee-um)

Sympodial

Light   Medium to bright

Temperature   Warm to cool

Flowering   Varies depending on species

Care   Easy to difficult, depending on species.

The genus *Dendrobium* is impossibly large. It contains over 1,000 species, found in a vast area stretching from Korea and Japan through the Malay region and from Indonesia to Australia and New Zealand. New Guinea is especially rich in dendrobiums; it is home to over 350 species.

Dendrobiums grow in climates that vary from steamy tropical lowlands to frosty mountain forests, and the flowering habits of the plants are often directly related to seasonal patterns. In order to flower, some species need cool conditions in the fall, some require a dry spell after the new growths mature, and others need a cool dry spell. The forms of dendrobium plants vary also. Some are compact,

pseudobulbous plants suitable for light gardens; others have thick canes several feet tall. To make sense of all this, the experts have divided the genus into sections with similar characteristics. Most popular dendrobiums fall into one of the following six sections.

Sections

Callista   These are evergreen plants, and most have pseudobulbs. The flower spikes, produced in the spring, are usually pendent, and carry flowers in shades of yellow, white, or lavender. Grow these types under intermediate conditions in summer. In winter they need cool nights and dry conditions. The youngest pseudobulbs should shrivel slightly during this winter treatment, but water them just enough to keep them from wasting away completely.

Dendrobium aggregatum, one of the most popular *Callista* species, is a 3- to 6-inch plant with spindle-shaped pseudobulbs and oblong, leathery leaves. The pendent orange-yellow flowers have large, rounded lips, and are

a little over 1 inch in diameter. A single spike may bear up to 30 flowers. Other species in this section include *Den. chrysotoxum, Den. densiflorum, Den. farmeri,* and *Den. thyrsiflorum.*

Spatulata   The species in this section are commonly called "antelope dendrobiums" because the flowers have an upright pair of twisted petals that resemble the horns of an antelope. The plants are evergreen and have no pseudobulbs. They need intermediate conditions throughout the year, but tolerate cool winters if kept dry. *Spatulata* species are easier to grow than some of the others because they flower without any special rest treatment. This section includes *Den. antennatum, canaliculatum, discolor, gouldii, johannis, lineale, stratiotes, strebloceras,* and *taurinum.*

Dendrobium   These species are deciduous, and most have drooping canes. The flowers are held near the ends of the mature, leafless canes. The plants need medium to bright

light and intermediate to cool temperatures in summer. They must have a cool dry winter for flowering; night temperatures should drop to between 40° and 50° F, and the plants should be watered very little and not fertilized at all.

Den. nobile, an upright species, is one of the most popular dendrobiums. Its fragrant flowers are about 3 inches across, and are usually borne in groups of three. The flower colors are variable, but some of the most popular forms have white petals with rose or mauve tips, and a ruffled lip with a deep maroon throat, grading into yellow and white. The edge of the lip may be tinged to match the petals. Other species in this large group include *Den. anosmum, chrysanthum, crassinode, falconeri, fimbriatum, findleyanum, friedricksianum, heterocarpum, loddigesii, moniliforme, parishii, primulinum, transparens,* and *wardianum.*

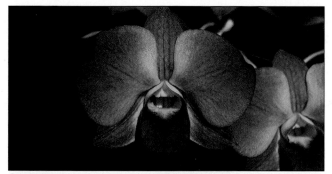

Dendrobium phalaenopsis 'Dawn', HCC/AOS

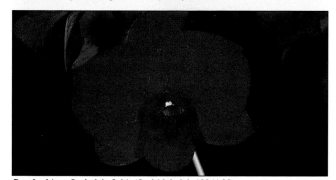

Dendrobium Orglade's Orbit 'Orchidglade', AM/AOS

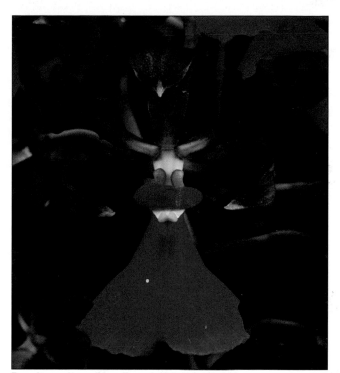

Encyclia cordigera 'Mem. Kenneth McBride', AM/AOS

Formosae The leaves are evergreen, and the narrow upright pseudobulbs have patches of black hair where the leaves join. The flowers are white, up to 4 inches across, and are marked with yellow, orange, green, or violet. The plants in this section require intermediate to cool conditions all year, and should dry out slightly in the winter. Species in this section include *Den. bellatulum, dearii, draconis, formosum, infundibulum, lowii, lyonii, margaritaceum, sanderae,* and *schuetzii.*

Latouria The plants are evergreen and have pseudobulbs. The flowers are usually yellow to green. A relatively easy group, these plants grow and flower well in intermediate to cool conditions. No special resting treatments are needed, but keep the plants on the dry side if the temperature drops into the cool range. *Dendrobium atroviolaceum, johnsoniae, macrophyllum,* and *spectabile* are some of the species in this group.

Phalaenanthe These plants may be evergreen or deciduous, depending on the conditions. Their pseudobulbs are tall and thin. The most popular species in this section, *Den. phalaenopsis,* bears flowers that are similar in many ways to those in the genus *Phalaenopsis.* They have a flattened shape and are arranged on the spike in two parallel rows. The individual flowers last a long time—up to six to eight weeks—and a plant may remain in bloom for three to four months. Flower colors of selections and hybrids range from pure white to deep reddish purple. Spikes are produced by new and old growths, beginning in early spring. In addition to their floral similarities, *Den. phalaenopsis* and *Phalaenopsis* species have similar cultural needs, requiring intermediate to warm temperatures throughout the year. *Den. phalaenopsis* will bloom in a light exposure at the low end of the medium range, alongside plants in the genus *Phalaenopsis.* The plants will,

however, produce sturdier growths and more flowers if given more light.

Phalaenanthe types need no special treatment to stimulate flowering, although overwatering will make a plant produce keikis instead of flowers. Other species in this section include *Den. affine, bigibbum, dicuphum,* and *williamsonianum.*

Hybrids

Most dendrobium hybrids are offspring of *Den. nobile* or *Den. phalaenopsis.* Of the *Den. nobile* hybrids, some of the most popular are the Yamamoto crosses, bred by Yamamoto Dendrobiums of Hawaii. These plants are now more commonly grown than the selections of *Den. nobile* species. Award-winning Yamamoto hybrids include: Utopia 'Messenger', São Paulo 'Memory', Hagaromo 'Spring Fuji', and Yukidaruma 'King'.

Some of the best *Den. phalaenopsis* hybrids are Anna Bibus, Hickam Deb, Marianne Bates, Ram Misra, Orglade's Orbit, and Lady Hamilton.

Epidendrum and Encyclia

(eh-pi-*den*-drum, en-*si*-clee-ah)

Sympodial

Light Medium

Temperature Warm to cool

Flowering All seasons, primarily spring-summer

Care Easy

The genus *Epidendrum* is also very large, but its culture is not as confusing as that of the dendrobiums. There are two main types of epidendrum species: those with reedlike stems and those with pseudobulbs. And, because orchids are never that simple, there are also some in-between forms. Some of the pseudobulbous epidendrums have been renamed by botanists, and are now properly placed in the genus *Encyclia,* though they may still be referred to as epidendrums in books and catalogs. Both names are listed in the descriptions following.

Encyclia tampensis

Epicattleya Honey 'Gene Dangler', HCC/AOS

Reed-stem epidendrums are important cut-flower orchids in Hawaii, but most grow too tall (up to 20 feet) and need too much light for indoor culture. Encyclias generally have compact growth habits and freely produce their fragrant flowers in home conditions. The shell-type encyclias, such as *Encyclia cochleata* and *Encyclia fragrans,* are particularly interesting because their "upside-down" flowers look like squid or octopuses. Luckily, the resemblance ends there; the flowers smell delightful. Encyclias require the same care as their relatives, the cattleyas.

Species

Encyclia adenocaula Straplike leaves arch from the pseudobulbs; the plant grows between 5 and 8 inches tall. The flower spikes hold many pink to rose-pink blooms with narrow petals. The long pointed lip has deep pink markings and an interesting winged column. It flowers in spring. Native to Mexico.

Encyclia cochleata (Epi. cochleatum) Of all the shell-type encyclias, this one looks most like an octopus. The plant is about 1 foot high, and fits neatly under lights. The shell-shaped lip is mostly green with purple and black stripes. The petals and sepals are yellow-green. It blooms from fall to spring, often more than once a year. It is native from Mexico to Venezuela and Cuba.

Encyclia cordigera (Epidendrum atropurpureum) This is a heavy plant with conical pseudobulbs and leathery, straplike leaves. It grows up to 2 feet tall. The fragrant flowers have brown to purple petals that curve forward at the tips, and the lip is creamy white with three bright pink splotches. In some forms, the entire lip is rosered. The flowers appear in spring and summer. Many varieties are available. Native

from Mexico to Peru and Brazil, this species is also found in Cuba.

Encyclia fragrans (Epi. fragrans) This is a stout species with erect growth between 10 and 15 inches tall. It has shell-type, spicily fragrant flowers (hence the species name *fragrans).* The petals and sepals are cream to yellow. The lip is the same color, candystriped with red. *Encyclia fragrans* blooms from May to June. It is native to Mexico and the West Indies to Ecuador, Peru, and Brazil.

Encyclia tampensis (Epi. tampense) This is the "butterfly orchid" of south Florida and the Bahama islands. The pseudobulbs cluster to form mats supporting leathery leaves up to 15 inches long. The 1-inch flowers are fragrant and pretty but not particularly spectacular. The sepals and petals are brownish green to apple green. The lip is white with a magenta spot. *Encyclia tampensis* usually blooms in spring or summer.

Epidendrum ciliare The upright pseudobulbs arising from a creeping rhizome make this plant look very much like a cattleya. It usually grows to about 1 foot tall. The fragrant flowers are about 5 inches across and have yellowish green petals and sepals. The lip is white and split into three lobes. The side lobes are fringed; the center lobe is narrow and straight. *Epi. ciliare* blooms in the winter and is very easy to grow. It occurs from Mexico and the West Indies to Colombia and Brazil.

Hybrids

Pseudobulbous epidendrums and encyclias are often crossed with cattleyas, their close relatives. These hybrids, called epicattleyas, are usually between 4 and 8 inches tall and produce 8- to 12-inch spikes of fragrant flowers. Their compact size makes them particularly well-suited to artificial light gardens.

Laelia pumila 'Sanbar Classic', HCC/AOS

Laelia purpurata 'Velvet Dusk', HCC/AOS

Laelia

(*lay*-lee-ah or *lie*-lee-ah)

Sympodial

Light   Medium to high

Temperature   Intermediate

Flowering   Varies

Care   Average

Laelias are closely related to cattleyas, an obvious fact if you see the plants side by side. Some laelias and cattleyas are so similar that it is sometimes difficult to discern the difference; botanists count pollinia: laelias have eight and cattleyas have four.

Laelias generally have large, showy flowers in vivid shades of orange, yellow, pink, purple, and white. With their ruffled, often brightly colored and patterned lips, they resemble cattleya flowers, but the petals and sepals of laelia flowers are usually narrower than those of cattleya. Laelia plants range in size from 3 inches to 2 feet. Compact species bear flowers on short spikes, but larger species may have 6-foot inflorescences crowded with blooms.

From a cultural standpoint, most laelias and cattleyas may be grown together. Although the majority of the laelias perform well in intermediate temperatures, some species do best in temperatures at the cool or warm ends of the intermediate range.

Species

Laelia anceps   One of the most widely grown laelia species, this plant's tightly clustered, waxy pseudobulbs are between 4 and 6 inches tall and have flattened sides. Each pseudobulb bears one leathery leaf up to 8 inches long. The flowers may be nearly 4 inches across, and are held on long stems. The sepals and petals are often pale rose-purple, but white forms are fairly common and quite beautiful. The outside of the three-lobed lip matches the petals, but the inside is bright crimson-purple, with yellow and red stripes in the throat. The flowers appear in winter and last about two months on the plant, but do not keep well when cut.

L. anceps is renowned for its endurance of high and low temperatures, withstanding spells as hot as 100° F and cold snaps when the temperature may drop to 20° F. It is native to Mexico.

L. pumila   This is a delightful miniature, easy to flower and sure to please. The oval pseudobulbs are about 1 inch long. The shiny leathery leaves reach about 5 inches tall. The flowers are large compared with the rest of the plant, averaging 3 to 4 inches across. The sepals and petals are a rich rosy purple. The lip is similarly colored and has a white throat. Many cultivars of *L. pumila* are available. These come in all shades of pink, and some are pure white. *L. pumila* flowers in the fall. It is found in Brazil.

L. purpurata   This is one of the largest laelias, reaching almost 20 inches tall. Considered some of the finest of the genus, the flowers are fragrant, long lasting, and up to 8 inches in diameter. The flower colors vary from pure white to bluish purple. The lip is usually marked with rich purple.

Hundreds of color forms are grown by collectors. Many hybrids are also available. It flowers in early summer, and is native to Brazil.

Hybrids

Laelia species interbreed freely, and many handsome interspecific hybrids have been produced.

The close relationship between laelias and cattleyas has not been overlooked by breeders, who have combined the brilliant colors of laelias with the pleasing shapes of cattleyas to produce remarkable laeliocattleyas. *L. anceps* has parented hundreds of fine hybrids, imparting desirable traits such as vigorous but compact growth, colorful flowers on long stems, and the ability to tolerate a wide range of temperatures.

Laelias may be crossed with brassavolas to form brassolaelias. Most commonly, laelia genes turn up in the trigeneric brassolaeliocattleya hybrids, of which there are hundreds.

Ludisia discolor 'Smitchen', CCM/AOS

Ludisia discolor var. *dawsoniana*

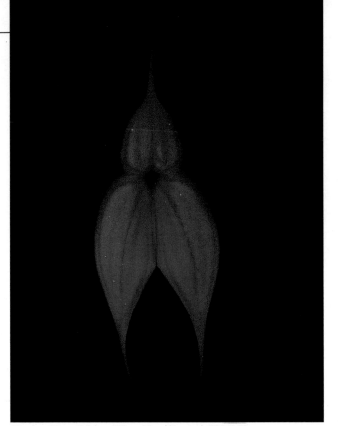

Masdevallia veitchiana 'Mem. Mary Chantry', FCC/AOS

Ludisia

(loo-*di*-see-ah)

Terrestrial

Light Low to medium

Temperature Intermediate to warm

Flowering Fall to winter

Care Average to difficult

Ludisias are the most popular of the "jewel orchids," a group of spreading, ground-dwelling plants. Most jewel orchids have insignificant flowers, but are grown for their beautiful iridescent foliage. Ludisia is also widely known as haemaria, its old name.

Species

This genus only contains one species, *Ludisia discolor.*

Ludisia discolor (Haemaria discolor) This is a low, spreading plant with 2- to 3-inch velvety maroon leaves that have contrasting metallic red or gold veins. The flowers are white with twisted yellow columns, measure about ¾ inch across, and are held on an upright stalk.

Ludisia discolor needs higher humidity and warmer temperatures than most other orchids—it makes an excellent terrarium plant. An old aquarium with a glass top is ideal. To provide a balance between high humidity and air circulation, leave the top of the terrarium partially open; a 2-inch gap is about right. Use a well-drained, humus-rich medium, such as a commercial terrestrial orchid mix or a homemade mixture of equal parts peat moss, perlite, and potting soil. The plants may be grown in pots within the terrarium or planted directly into growing medium in the bottom of the terrarium. If you grow the plants in pots, surround them with moist peat or sphagnum moss to maintain the humidity.

Ludisia grows best in temperatures 75° to 85° F. If the plants look healthy but refuse to grow, try raising the temperature inside the terrarium with heating cables (see page 20). The heating cables will also increase the humidity. *Ludisia discolor* is native to Indochina and from Burma to Indonesia.

Masdevallia

(maz-de-*val*-lee-a)

Sympodial

Light Low to medium

Temperature Most cool, some intermediate

Flowering Varies, most spring to summer

Care Average to difficult

The showiest parts of a masdevallia flower are the sepals; in this genus the petals are tiny structures nestled in the center of the flower. The sepals join at the base and narrow toward the tips, often into long tails, making the flowers of some species resemble kites. Most forms have distinctly triangular or tubular flowers. The flower colors include pure white, green, and brownish black, but the most popular species are orange to red. Flower sizes range from about 1 inch to as long as 10 inches. Some are pendent, others are erect.

Masdevallias are true cloud forest orchids, requiring constant moisture. They have no pseudobulbs—the fleshy leaves are borne on tiny stems sprouting from small rhizomes—and thus cannot endure periods without water. Most are from high elevations (between 6,000 and 12,000 feet) and need cool conditions, but a few species will grow in intermediate temperatures.

Although masdevallias need lots of humidity, excess water on the plant causes a fungus infection that rots the leaves where they join the stem. Don't compensate for low humidity with frequent mistings or waterings. If your plants do succumb to the fungus, treat them with a fungicide containing benomyl and improve the ventilation.

Species

If you live in an area with cool summers and are able to provide plenty of humidity, you can grow any of the masdevallias. *Masdevallia veitchiana,* a beauty with bright orange flowers covered with tiny fluorescent purple hairs, grows wild in the ruins of Machu Picchu in the Peruvian Andes. *Masd. coccinea,* another plant from the Andes, has a number of different color forms, including scarlet, magenta, yellow, and white.

Masdevalia infracta 'Devine', CCM/AOS

Miltonia clowesii 'Warren Street', CHM/AOS

In areas with intermediate temperatures the following species will probably be more successful:

Masd. floribunda A small tufted plant, this masdevallia grows to about 4 inches tall. Named for its abundant flowers, it blooms from early summer to early fall. The pale yellow blossoms are about 1 inch across and are spotted with brown or purple. The tips of the sepals have a reddish tinge. It is native to Mexico, Guatemala, Honduras, and Belize.

Masd. infracta This plant's tufts of leaves are taller, reaching up to 8 inches. The sepals are joined at their bases to form a bell, then narrow abruptly into three outwardly curving tails. The flower colors vary but most are pale yellow with deep red to purple markings. *Masd. infracta* blooms from spring to summer. It is found in Brazil and Peru.

Masd. peristeria This is an unusual species with leaves about 5 inches long. The 4- to 5-inch flowers open wide and are green with purple spots. The tails are relatively short (about 1½ inches) and have a yellow tinge. It flowers from April through June and is native to Colombia.

Masd. tovarensis One of the most popular masdevallias, *Masd. tovarensis* is noted for its showy flowers that look like kites. The plant grows in clumps reaching from 4 to 7 inches tall. Each long stem bears several translucent white flowers with greenish tails. The lower sepals are wide and joined for most of their length; and the upper sepal consists of little other than a narrow, upright spur. Native to Venezuela, its blooming season is winter.

Hybrids

Masdevallias were all the rage in England in the late 1800s, and many growers crossed the species sent to them by New World plant explorers. Around the turn of the century, interest in masdevallia breeding waned and few new hybrids were made for more than 50 years. In the last few decades, however, several orchid firms in the United States have taken up masdevallia breeding and produced some exquisite new hybrids. These breeders are combining the large flower size and bright colors of the cool-growing species with the vigorous growth and abundant blooming of the intermediate species to create stunning hybrids that are much easier to grow than their parents.

One of the first of these new hybrids was *Masd.* Marguerite, a cross of *Masd. veitchiana* and *Masd. infracta*. According to the growers, *Masd. infracta* gives the plants vigor and the ability to tolerate intermediate temperatures, but the flowers look like those of *Masd. veitchiana*—orange with a purplish red band of tiny hairs down the centers of the sepals.

Masd. Angel Frost, a hybrid of *Masd. strobelii* and *Masd. veitchiana*, has two lovely forms. Both have large, open, yellow-orange flowers, but some have the the tiny white hairs of *Masd. strobelii* and others have the purple hairs of *Masd. veitchiana*.

Miltonia

(mil-*toh*-nee-a)

Sympodial

Light Low to medium

Temperature Colombian: cool; Brazilian: intermediate

Flowering Most summer to fall

Care Average to difficult

Miltonias are the well-known "pansy orchids," plants with large flat flowers that look very much like the flowers in the popular genus *Viola*. Some miltonia flowers are lightly fragrant. A part of the subtribe Oncidiinae, the approximately twenty species of Miltonias are distinguished from their relatives in the *Odontoglossum, Oncidium,* and *Brassia* genera by differences in their flowers—very minor differences in some cases. When not in flower, the thin leaves and flattened pseudobulbs of miltonias are so similar to those of species in related genera that it is sometimes difficult to tell the plants apart.

There are two types of miltonias, differing in flower form and cultural require-

Miltonia spectabilis var. *moreliana* 'Elizabeth Grenis', AM/AOS

Miltonia vexillaria 'Giselle', AM/AOS

ments. The ones with the flat pansy-type flowers grow in high, cool areas of Colombia and nearby countries. These are now technically grouped in the genus *Miltoniopsis*. Flower colors in this group range from white to pink, with splotches of crimson to magenta. These plants do best in light intensities in the 1,000 to 1,500 footcandle range, about the same intensity required by phalaenopsis plants. They need cool night temperatures and are sensitive to daytime temperatures over 80° F.

The flowers of the other type, the Brazilian miltonias, don't resemble pansies; they look more like odontoglossums, blooming in shades of yellow and green marked with brown, purple, or red. They prefer medium light intensities (1,500 to 3,000 footcandles) and slightly warmer temperatures than do the Colombian species.

Miltonias of both types sunburn easily. If the plants are getting enough light, the leaves will be light green, lighter than you may think is healthy if you compare them to most other plants. A slight

tinge of pink indicates that the plants are receiving as much light as they will tolerate. Because sunburn is actually caused by high leaf temperatures, experienced growers shade their plants (or move them farther from the window) during hot spells. They also feel the leaves on sunny days to make sure they are not much warmer than the surrounding air.

Despite the presence of their water-storing pseudobulbs, miltonias can't withstand periods of dryness. Water them as you would cymbidiums, keeping the medium moist—but not soggy—at all times. A potting mix of fine fir bark, amended with sphagnum moss, perlite, and a little charcoal provides a good balance of water and air for these moisture-loving plants. If the new leaves emerge pleated, the plant is not getting enough water. Increased watering won't flatten them out (they will always look like accordions) but the next leaves should be smooth.

The flowers of the Colombian species last from two

weeks to two months on the plant, but wither quickly when cut. Brazilian miltonias make fine cut flowers.

Brazilian Species

Miltonia clowesii The sepals and petals of these 2- to 3-inch fragrant flowers are chestnut brown with yellow markings. The lip is shaped like an inverted spade, and is white at the bottom and violet to purple with yellow markings at the top. The plants grow between 1 and 1½ feet tall, and bloom from summer to fall on 2-foot spikes. Each spike holds 7 to 10 flowers.

Milt. regnellii The white sepals and petals of this species are sometimes tinted with rose. The broad, slightly undulating lip is light pink streaked with deeper pink. At the center of the lip is a yellow structure called the callus. The flowers are generally between 2 and 3 inches across. Three to five flowers are borne on each 2-foot spike. The plant reaches 1 to 1½ feet tall. It flowers from summer to fall.

Milt. spectabilis The growth habit of this miltonia is a bit unruly. The pseudobulbs are spaced about 1 inch apart and are quickly forced over the edges of the pot by the rapid growth of the rhizome. But the flowers are splendid. Borne one to a stem, they have white sepals and petals, sometimes with a rosy tinge toward the base. The white lip is large and spreading, and has reddish purple lines radiating from the yellow callus at the center. In the variety *moreliana*, the sepals and petals match the deep reddish purple markings in the lip. The plants can be very floriferous, putting on a wonderful show in late summer.

Colombian Species

Milt. vexillaria (Miltoniopsis vexillaria) This popular Colombian species appears in the pedigree of many hybrids. The plants have erect, sturdy growth to about 1 foot tall. The flowers are large—sometimes more than 4 inches across—and dazzlingly showy. The bright rose and white sepals and petals

Miltonia × Bluntii

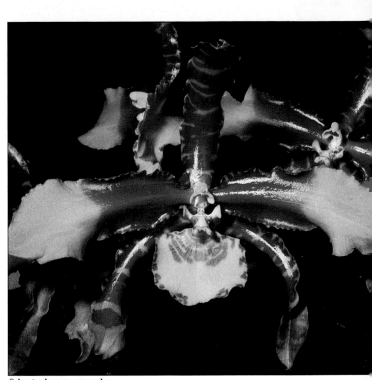

Odontoglossum grande

are small in relation to the richly colored lip, which spreads out magnificently and splits into two fat lobes. The lip is mostly white, variously streaked with red and yellow. *Milt. vexillaria* flowers in the spring and summer.

Brazilian Hybrids

In addition to increasing the number and size of the flowers, breeders of Brazilian miltonias are creating hybrids that will tolerate a wide range of temperatures. Many new hybrids are registered each year, most containing genes of the following hybrid parents.

Milt. Anne Warne is the first registered Brazilian miltonia hybrid, the result of a cross made in 1949 of *Milt.* × Bluntii and *Milt. spectabilis* var. *moreliana.* Its flowers are a deep purple and are held singly just above the foliage.

Brazilian miltonias easily form natural hybrids; *Milt.* × Bluntii is one of the most important. A cross of *Milt. clowesii* and *Milt. spectabilis,* the foliage of *Milt.* × Bluntii closely resembles that of *Milt. spectabilis.* The fragrant flow-

ers are about 3 inches long. The sepals and petals are light yellow with reddish brown blotches. The lip is similar in shape and color to the lip of *Milt. spectabilis,* but it does not come to a point. The plant blooms from summer to fall.

Colombian Hybrids

These flowers have beautiful rounded shapes and bright combinations of red, pink, white, and yellow. The markings at the base of the lip, called the "mask" by breeders, are intricate and striking. In some of these hybrids, such as *Milt.* Celle, the mask is a splash of colors; hybridizers call these "waterfall masks." In the future, breeders hope to combine the traits of these cool-growing beauties with the best of the Brazilian hybrids.

Intergeneric hybrids

Miltonias have been crossed with brassias, odontoglossums, oncidiums, and cochliodas. These hybrids vary in their temperature requirements, and are described under the next genus, *Odontoglossum.*

Odontoglossum

(oh-don-toh-*gloss*-um)

Sympodial

Light Medium

Temperature Cool

Flowering Varies with species

Care Average to difficult

The genus *Odontoglossum* is a large one, containing approximately 300 species. Botanists have tidied up the genus by moving some of the species to the genus *Rossioglossum,* but these are still commonly called odontoglossums.

The exquisite inflorescences of these plants are produced from the bases of the flattened pseudobulbs, and are usually erect and arching. The flowers are often large and showy, and come in shades of white, yellow, or green, marked with purple or brown blotches.

Their showy flowers have made odontoglossums very popular with hobbyists, despite the plants' sometimes exacting temperature requirements. Most species live high in the Andes mountains, where they are continually

bathed in cool moist fog. They thrive in nighttime low temperatures of 45° F and daytime highs of 60° F—conditions similar to those required by cymbidiums. Outside of the Pacific Northwest, most areas of the United States are just too warm for these plants. Some of the best-known species in this group are *Odontoglossum crispum, Odm. luteo-purpureum,* and *Odm. odoratum.* Over 1,000 varieties of *Odm. crispum* have been named.

Odontoglossums should not be allowed to dry out completely between waterings. Many growers use a mixture containing 1 part coarse sand, 1 part shredded peat, 1 part coarse perlite, and 4 parts fine bark to satisfy the plants' requirement for a moist, well-drained medium.

Repot only when necessary to replace the growing medium; odontoglossums do not grow well if their roots are frequently disturbed. When repotting, remove the old, leafless pseudobulbs with flame-sterilized shears. Check the cut surface of the pseudobulb

Miltassia Aztec 'Purple Star' HCC/AOS

Odontobrassia Inca 'Royal Indian', HCC/AOS

Vuylstekeara Cambria 'Plush', FCC/AOS–RHS

for rot. Rotted areas are light to dark brown; healthy tissue is white. Remove all rotten growth and sear the cut surfaces of the healthy growths with the heated blade of the shears before repotting them.

Species

A few odontoglossums native to lower elevations will tolerate cool (rather than cold) temperatures. These plants need night temperatures in the cool to intermediate range, but don't do very well if the day temperatures climb above 70° F for long periods.

Odm. pulchellum Given time, this plant will form a large, handsome clump about 15 inches tall. The white flowers are rounded and fragrant. At the center of each flower is a yellow callus with reddish brown spots. Three to ten flowers are borne on a slim, erect stalk in the spring. *Odm. pulchellum* is native to Mexico, Guatemala, El Salvador, and Costa Rica.

Rossioglossum grande (*Odm. grande*) Popularly called the "tiger orchid," its waxy flowers are anywhere from 5 to 9 inches across. This plant gets its common name from its coloring: golden yellow with reddish brown bands and flecks. The callus looks like a fat little doll. The plant grows to about 15 inches tall and blooms anytime from fall to spring. It is found in Mexico and Guatemala.

Hybrids

Hybrids of *Odontoglossum* with related genera such as *Oncidium* and *Miltonia* are much more adaptable to intermediate temperatures than are the *Odontoglossum* species and their hybrids. In addition to growing well in a wide range of temperatures, the intergeneric hybrids have large flowers with interesting shapes and unusual colors.

Although they are much more adaptable than the species from which they were bred, these intergeneric hybrids do have temperature preferences. The hybrids in the following man-made genera adapt to intermediate conditions. Some of these hybrids don't contain odontoglossum

genes, but are listed here for easy comparison.

Aliceara (Brassia × Miltonia × Oncidium)
Brassidium (Brassia × Oncidium)
Colmanara (Miltonia × Odontoglossum × Oncidium)
Miltassia (Miltonia × Brassia)
Miltonidium (Miltonia × Oncidium)
Odontocidium (Odontoglossum × Oncidium)
Wilsonara (Odontoglossum × Cochlioda × Oncidium)

Of these, the aliceareas, brassidiums, miltonidiums, and miltassias do fairly well in warm temperatures. Many can be grown successfully in south Florida or in other areas where high summer temperatures overwhelm odontoglossums and the cool-growing hybrids. Beauty has not been compromised in the creation of warmth-tolerant hybrids; many have received awards. One of the finest aliceareas, producing 6-inch cream and brown flowers with large ruffled lips, is *Aliceara* Hawaiian

Delight 'Sunshine' (HCC/AOS). Brassidiums, such as *Brassidium* Florida Gem 'Sylvia' (HCC/AOS) have the starry shapes of brassias and the yellow and brown markings of oncidiums.

The following hybrids often have cool-growing species in their backgrounds and thus grow better in cool conditions.

Vuylstekeara (Miltonia × Cochlioda × Odontoglossum)
Odontioda (Odontoglossum × Cochlioda)
Odontobrassia (Odontoglossum × Brassia)
Odontonia (Odontoglossum × Miltonia)

Some of the finest of these hybrids were produced before the second world war and are now available as mericlones. *Vuylstekeara* Cambria 'Plush' (FCC/AOS-RHS) is one of the most famous. It has a superb burgundy flower with a large, ruffled lip marked with intricate white patterns. Another vuylstekeara awarded an FCC/AOS is *Vuylstekeara* Edna 'Stamperland'. Excellent prewar odontonia hybrids are also readily available.

Oncidium crispum 'J & L', AM/AOS

Oncidium splendidum 'Robert', HCC/AOS

Oncidium

(on-*sid*-ee-um)

Sympodial

Light Medium to high

Temperature Intermediate

Flowering Varies

Care Easy

Dancing, flickering, fanciful, fairylike—*Oncidium* has probably inspired more poetic language than any other orchid genus. The common names of *Oncidium* species refer to anything from dancing dolls to mule's ears, a reflection of the variety to be found in the approximately 500 species that make up this genus. The robust, shimmering sprays of the larger oncidiums are dramatic and elegant, and the dainty spikes of the smaller species are delightful. Yellow and brown are the predominant flower colors in the genus, but white, purple, pink, and green hues are also found in some of the species. The flowers all have warty protuberances on the crest of the lip, a trait that distinguishes the genus and creates an interesting focal point in the flower.

The size and shape of oncidium plants vary tremendously. The smallest species are the equitant oncidiums (so called for their lengthwise folded leaves), characterized by *Oncidium triquetrum*. These plants have pointed, three-sided leaves 2 to 3 inches long. They grow on the branches of trees and shrubs on Caribbean islands, but also thrive on tree fern slabs or in small baskets of lava rock in orchid growers' homes.

Other species, such as *Onc. ampliatum,* have pseudobulbs and thin leaves. These plants are known for their wonderfully long inflorescences that bear perfectly spaced flowers on well-formed branches. A large specimen may produce a 6- to 8-foot spray bearing hundreds of flowers.

Onc. splendidum is an example of a third type. These species have thick oval upright leaves 4 to 8 inches tall, and are thus called the "mule's ear" oncidiums. They tolerate lower humidity than most orchids, but need bright light to bloom well. Some have fragrant flowers.

Unlike their relatives in the genera *Odontoglossum* and *Miltonia, Oncidium* species are generally easy to grow, adapting well to intermediate temperatures and tolerating an occasional missed watering without damage.

Species

Onc. ampliatum The pseudobulbs of this species are large and rounded, reminiscent of turtle shells. The leaves are about 15 inches long and may be up to 5 inches wide. Brilliant yellow flowers, about 1 inch across, are borne on arching sprays up to 4 feet long. The lip crest at the center of the flower is white with red spots. *Onc. ampliatum* usually blooms in spring. It is native to Guatemala, Venezuela, and Bolivia.

Onc. carthagenense One of the "mule's ear" oncidiums, this species has thick upright leaves between 6 and 24 inches long that are spotted with tiny dots of reddish brown. The flower spikes are up to 5 feet tall and bear numerous ruffled purple and white flowers, usually about

1 inch across. Its blooming season is summer. Wild plants may be found in southern Florida, the West Indies, and from Mexico to Venezuela and Brazil.

Onc. cheirophorum This is a charming little plant with shiny, tightly clustered pseudobulbs. The thin leaves are short; the plants reach a maximum height of about 4 inches. The flowers are vivid yellow, very waxy, and deliciously fragrant. They are borne in dense clusters on 6-inch spikes. The blooming season lasts from fall through winter and the species occurs in Nicaragua, Costa Rica, Panama, and in the highlands of Colombia.

Onc. crispum The form of *Onc. crispum* flowers is different from that of most other oncidiums. The large ruffled petals and huge dorsal sepal are nearly as big as the lip. The sepals and petals are coppery red to greenish brown. The lip is the same color, with a yellow patch at the base and crest. The crest is decorated with warty red protuberances.

Oncidium tigrinum

Oncidium papilio 'Robert Parke', AM/AOS

Onc. crispum grows best in temperatures at the cool end of the intermediate range. The oval leaves are borne two to three to a pseudobulb, and reach about 9 inches long. It flowers from fall to winter, and is native to Brazil.

Onc. luridum A large "mule's ear" type, *Onc. luridum* has stout leaves over 2½ feet tall. The branching flower stalk is about 4 feet tall, bearing showy flowers in white with rose markings. The lip is tinged with orange and the crest is yellow with a pattern of orange lines. It flowers in spring. It is native to south Florida and the West Indies, and from Mexico to Peru.

Onc. macranthum This is one of the microchilum (small-lipped) oncidiums, a group of species with large flowers in brown and gold with sharply pointed lips. The flowers of *Onc. macranthum* are probably the largest in the genus, spreading to 4 inches across. They are held on a branched, vining stalk an incredible 8 to 12 feet long. If the inflorescence is trained on a wire hoop as it develops, it will be more manageable, and, when the flowers open, they will form a wreath of blossoms. The sepals of these flowers are brown, the petals gold. The complex lip has violet side lobes and a yellow midlobe. The crest of the lip has a cushion of white spikes tipped with purple. This species needs temperatures at the cool end of the intermediate range. It blooms in early summer. It is found in Ecuador and in the highlands of Peru.

Onc. papilio Often a center of attention at orchid shows, the flower of *Onc. papilio* looks like a large hovering insect. The dorsal sepal and petals are long and narrow, curving up and forward like antennae. The lateral sepals and lip are yellow with brown markings. The lip crest is fascinating; use a hand lens to get a close look at the callus at the center—it looks like a mask. The 10- to 15-inch flower spikes produce new flowers at the tip. Just as the oldest flower fades a new one opens to take its place. This can go on throughout the year. *Onc. papilio* is native to Peru, Venezuela, Trinidad, Colombia, and Ecuador.

Onc. sphacelatum This robust species has 6-inch pseudobulbs and its leaves grow to more than 2 feet long. The golden yellow and brown flowers are held on an upright, branched inflorescence. The side branches are longest at the bottom and shortest at the top, giving the stalk of flowers an appealing symmetry similar to that of an espalier. Flowering from November to June, this species is native to a large area in tropical America, including Mexico, Honduras, Guatemala, and El Salvador.

Onc. splendidum One of the largest of the "mule's ear" oncidiums (see page 81), this species has leaves about 3 feet tall. The showy flowers are 3 inches across, with lemon yellow and brown sepals and petals. The large, clear yellow lip is smooth and rounded. This species blooms spring to early summer, and occurs in Guatemala and Honduras.

Onc. tigrinum The greenish yellow and brown sepals of these flowers provide a dark background for the striking yellow lip. The pronounced isthmus of the lip (the narrowed portion in the center) lends it an asymmetrical dumbbell shape. The fragrant flowers are about 2½ inches across and are carried on 2-foot spikes. The plant grows to about 1½ feet tall and will flower in most conditions. Look for new flower spikes in the fall. It is found in Mexico.

Onc. triquetrum The thick, three-sided leaves of this equitant species are arranged in a fan about 3 inches tall. The petals and lip of the 1-inch flowers are white, dotted with maroon. The contrasting sepals are greenish brown, lighter around the edges. Five to fifteen flowers are borne on each 7-inch spike. It usually blooms in the summer, but some specimens are practically everblooming. Don't cut the spikes after flowering; they often branch and bloom again. It is native to Jamaica.

Paphiopedilum callosum 'Rayber', HCC/AOS

Paphiopedilum bellatulum 'Vasco', AM/AOS

Onc. varicosum The name "dancing dolls" is applied to other oncidiums, but it describes this species best of all. The bright yellow and brown flowers perform in troupes of up to 200 on lacily branched stems. A single inflorescence may be up to 5 feet long. The pseudobulbous plant is about 1 foot tall. The variety *rogersii* is most commonly grown. Its flowers are larger than most (about 2 inches across). The dancing dolls' show premiers in the fall and continues into the winter. *Onc. varicosum* is native to Brazil.

Hybrids

Aside from interspecific crosses of equitants, most oncidium breeding involves intergeneric hybrids. Oncidiums don't have enough colors to keep an orchid breeder interested for long, but they do contribute their excellent flower count and vigorous growth habit to hybrids made with odontoglossums, miltonias, and brassias. These hybrids are discussed with the odontoglossum hybrids on page 80.

Paphiopedilum

(paff-ee-oh-*ped*-i-lum)

Sympodial

Light Low to medium, depending on species

Temperature Intermediate to cool, depending on species

Flowering Generally fall to spring

Care Very easy to difficult

Paphiopedilums differ from other orchids in both the appearance of the plants and their flowers. One of the most obvious features that sets the flowers apart is the lip, which is modified into a pouch like a cup. This pouch suggests the name "lady's slipper," a common name applied to paphiopedilums and their relatives in the subfamily Cypripedioideae.

Another very showy part of a paphiopedilum flower is the dorsal (uppermost) sepal, which is usually shaped like an upside-down heart and colorfully marked with distinct lines or spots. The two lower sepals are fused into one, and may be almost completely hidden behind the pouch. The long, narrow petals stick straight out at the sides of the flower, or may hang down like a long moustache. Tufts of black hairs sprout from the upper edges of the petals in some species. All of the flower parts are thick and waxy, taking on the texture of rubbery plastic in the modern hybrids.

Green, brown, white, and pink hues predominate in the species; the hybrids may also contain vivid shades of red and purple. These colors may be subtly blended or patterned in bold stripes and spots. The flowers are usually borne singly atop thick stalks, but a few species bear as many as six flowers on a single stalk.

Paphiopedilums also have a unique growth habit. Unlike most orchids, which live in the bright sunlight of the treetops, paphiopedilums are terrestrials, living in the shade of the forest floor. This environment is always moist, so these plants have no water-storing stems or pseudobulbs. Their leathery leaves join at the base of the plant, forming fans of three to seven leaves. The leaves are pure green or mottled with light and dark green.

Although paphiopedilums grow on the ground and are classified as terrestrials, their roots usually do not penetrate the soil, but ramble instead through the moist, well-aerated humus on the surface. You can simulate this root environment with a variety of potting mediums; fine fir bark amended with a little perlite is a tried-and-true mixture. Plants should be watered frequently enough to keep them moist but not soggy. Plastic pots are generally used to help retain moisture.

When watering paphiopedilums, avoid splashing water into the growing points and leaf axils. If water collects and remains in these places for long, a bacterial rot can kill the growing points and young leaves. Overzealous misting can also cause bacterial infections. Paphiopedilums are also sensitive to salt accumulation. Leach the medium occasionally with plain water and don't overfertilize.

Green-leaved paphiopedilums and mottled-leaved paphiopedilums have different

Paphiopedilum fairieanum 'Maj', AM/AOS

Paphiopedilum venustum 'McQuerry', HCC/AOS

temperature requirements. Species and hybrids with green leaves generally need cool night temperatures, especially in the fall when the flower buds are developing. Plants with mottled leaves bloom freely in intermediate night temperatures. Day temperatures between 70° and 80° F are ideal for both types.

Both types of paphiopedilum also do well in light intensities ranging from 800 to 1,200 footcandles. The light intensity should be at the low end of the range in the summer when temperatures are high so that the plants don't dry out too quickly. Leaf yellowing may be a sign of too much light. The foliage of the green-leaved forms should be a medium green; the darker patches in mottled-leaf forms should be deep green. Paphiopedilums are excellent orchids for fluorescent light gardens.

Their undemanding light and temperature requirements and free-blooming habits make the mottled-leaved paphiopedilums some of the best orchids for the beginning windowsill gardener. Not only do

the plants bloom frequently and with no special treatment, but also the flowers last in perfect form on the plant or in a vase for at least a month; some last up to three months. Their attractive foliage makes them decorative even when they are not in bloom.

Paphiopedilums are best allowed to grow into large specimen plants. They may be divided if they grow too large, die out in the center, or if you simply want more plants. Break (rather than cut) the plants apart, creating divisions with at least three growths. Paphiopedilums don't respond well to meristem culture; most of the plants on the market are seedlings or very old cultivars that have been multiplied through division.

Mottled-Leaved Species

Paphiopedilum bellatulum The dark green leaves of this unusual species are sparingly mottled on their upper surfaces and have purple spots below. The inflorescence is so short that the flowers are borne right on top

of the leaves. The entire flower is white or pale yellow and is liberally spotted with purplish brown. Unlike those of most other paphiopedilums, the petals of this species are rounded and are larger than the dorsal sepal. It blooms in spring, and is native to Burma and Thailand.

Paph. callosum The leaves of this species are a light bluish green with darker mottling. The flowers are about 4 inches across and are very long-lived. The large, rounded dorsal sepal is white and green with purple streaks. The petals point downward at 45-degree angles. They are greenish at the base and suffused with purple at the tips. The lip is brownish purple. This species flowers in spring to summer. It is native to Thailand, Laos, and Cambodia.

Paph. sukhakulii This species' leaves are dark green, mottled with light green. The dorsal sepal is pale green with well-defined lines of much darker green. The petals are stiff, nearly flat, and point slightly downward. They are pale green, spotted all over

with deep purple. The lip of this exotic and unusual species is pale green, mottled and veined with purple. The flowers are produced in the summer. It occurs in Thailand.

Paph. venustum The leaves of this species are particularly attractive. The upper surfaces are dark green with pale mottling; the undersides are deep purplish green. The dorsal sepal is white with green lines. The petals are similarly colored at their bases, but the ends look as if they have been dipped in red lacquer and their wavy edges bristle with black hairs. The lip is orange to bronze and is veined with green. It blossoms from late winter to early summer, and grows wild in Nepal, Bangladesh, and India.

Green-Leaved Species

Paph. fairieanum This small plant has ornate flowers about 2½ inches across. The dorsal sepal is white with violet lines and netting. It is very large in proportion to the rest of the flower and has wavy edges. The upward-curling petals have the same pattern and

Paphiopedilum Maudiae 'Dorothy Ann', AM/AOS

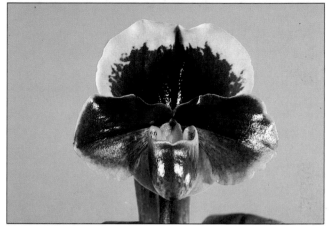

Paphiopedilum Maudiae 'Pinot Noir', AM/AOS

Paphiopedilum Sioux 'Teal', AM/AOS

coloration as the lip but with the addition of a greenish tinge. The green and violet lip has purple veins. It blooms from summer to early fall. *Paph. fairieanum* occurs in India.

Paph. insigne Although this species sometimes bears two flowers on a stem, most of the time it produces a single 4- to 5-inch blossom. The brownish tinge and shiny surface of the apple green flowers make them look as if they've been varnished. The dorsal sepal is yellow to light green with slightly darker green lines and brown to purple spots. The undulating petals and helmet-shaped lip have a color scheme similar to that of the dorsal sepal, but with more brown or purple. It may flower at any time from fall to spring. Like most of the other green-leaf paphiopedilums, this species is native to India and Nepal.

Paph. philippinense The dorsal sepals of these flowers, pleasingly triangular, are white with reddish brown lines. The long, twisted reddish purple petals are the most striking aspects of the flower, dangling to 6 inches below the center of the flower. The lip is yellow with faint brown markings, a stunning contrast to the rest of the blossom. It blooms from summer to autumn, and is native to the Philippines.

Hybrids

Paph. Maudiae is without a doubt the best paphiopedilum—some say the best orchid—for the beginner. Its beautiful mottled foliage, superb flowers, and ability to thrive in low light and average home temperatures make this hybrid one of the beginning orchid grower's best bets.

Paph. Maudiae was first produced in 1900 by a cross of the *album* (white and green) forms of *Paph. lawrenceanum* and *Paph. callosum.* These *album* forms of *Paph.* Maudiae, still popular and widely available, have white dorsal sepals with clearly defined, bright green veins. The white-tipped petals are light green with veins of darker green. The pouch is yellow

green with faint green venation. The flowers are borne on long stems above the light and dark green mottled foliage, and last from two to three months. *Paph.* Maudiae 'Dorothy Ann' is a typical *album* hybrid.

Not all *Paph.* Maudiae hybrids have green and white flowers. Two other color forms, *coloratum* and *vinicolorum* (usually called vinicolor for short) are also available. The *coloratum* forms, produced by crossing normally pigmented *Paph. lawrenceanum* and *Paph. callosum* plants, have red flowers with darker red veins. Tufts of jet black hairs sprout from the upper edges of the petals. 'Los Osos', 'St. Francis', and 'Diamond Jubilee' are excellent cultivars of the *coloratum* forms; all bear Awards of Merit from the American Orchid Society.

The richly hued vinicolor forms are the latest of the Maudiae hybrids. Their flowers are a deep burgundy; some are nearly black with purplered pigments. The heavy coloration comes from two cultivars of *Paph. callosum,* 'Jac' and

'Sparkling Burgundy'. In order to be classed as a vinicolor and not just a deeply hued *coloratum,* the flower must be a clear purple-red without a trace of brown, and the tip of the pouch must be nearly black. Unfortunately, excellent vinicolor cultivars are very expensive and are likely to remain so until growers develop methods to clone them through meristem culture.

Paph. Maudiae has been crossed with species paphiopedilums to produce stunning results. *Paph.* Faire-Maude, a cross of *Paph.* Maudiae and *Paph. fairieanum,* has been best described as a Maudiae with an oriental look. *Paph.* Makuli *(Paph. sukhakulii* × *Paph.* Maudiae) has the straight, simple lines of *Paph. sukhakulii* and the easygoing cultural requirements of *Paph.* Maudiae.

There are many hybrids in the green-leaved group, such as *Paph.* Sioux 'Teal'. Often grown for cut flowers, they tend to have extremely large, rounded flowers with a heavy, rubbery texture.

Phalaenopsis lueddemanniana 'Jo-San', HCC/AOS

Phalaenopsis amabilis 'Truford', AM/AOS

Phalaenopsis schilleriana 'Classic', HCC/AOS

Phalaenopsis

(fal-en-*op*-sis)

Monopodial

Light Low

Temperature Warm to intermediate

Flowering Fall to winter, some year-round.

Care Easy

How could such sublimely beautiful orchids be so easy to grow? Phalaenopsis orchids, commonly called "moth orchids" for their enchanting white flowers, are some of the very easiest for the beginner. Like the mottled-leaved paphiopedilums, phalaenopsis plants thrive in intermediate temperatures and low light. Their low, compact growth makes them ideal windowsill plants, and they fit perfectly under fluorescent lights. Add to this easy culture their attractive foliage and beautiful long-lasting blossoms and it is easy to see why they've become so popular.

Unlike most of the orchids mentioned in this book, phalaenopsis plants are monopodial, producing new leaves at the top of the plant year after year, rather than producing new growths from the base. In theory, this should make them grow taller and taller without spreading out but, because the lower leaves usually die and fall off as the plant grows taller, most growers "top" their plants and repot the upper portion before the plant reaches 1 foot.

Although the leafy part of a phalaenopsis plant is low and compact, the flower spikes of the popular species and hybrids are erect and arching, usually reaching between 2 and 3 feet tall. Botanically speaking, the largest and most popular moth orchids belong in a section of the genus *Phalaenopsis* also called Phalaenopsis. The species in this section include *Phal. amabilis, Phal. schilleriana,* and *Phal. stuartiana.*

The flowers in section Phalaenopsis have broad, thin petals that are usually larger than the sepals, sometimes covering the space between them and giving the flowers their graceful rounded appearance. Another feature that distinguishes the plants in this section is the lip, which is tipped with a pair of appendages that resemble antennae or horns. The blooming season is usually from winter to spring. When the flowers fade, cut the stalk just below the node that produced the first flower. If all goes well, the stem will branch and flower again. In this way plants can be kept in bloom for months.

The plants in another section, Stauroglottis, have foliage similar to that of plants in section Phalaenopsis, but the flowers are thicker, star-shaped, and borne in short drooping inflorescences. Although these plants are not grown as commonly as are the large hybrids, their bright colors and generous blooming habits should earn them a place in any orchid collection. Most of these species have their peak flowering season in the summer, but they keep producing new flowers at the ends of the inflorescences for years, a wonderful phenomenon called "successive flowering." As the flowers bloom, fade, and fall off, their bracts remain on the flower stem, giving old inflorescences an interesting saw-toothed appearance. Eventually, the end of the inflorescence will stop producing flowers and turn brown. The entire inflorescence can then be removed.

Like paphiopedilums, phalaenopsis plants don't have pseudobulbs, so they are more sensitive to low humidity or a dry growing medium than are the pseudobulbous orchids such as cattleyas. Keep the bark moist, and try to maintain a high humidity.

Also like paphiopedilums, phalaenopsis orchids can become infected with a bacterial rot if water stands in the center of the plant or in the leaf axils for long periods of time. This rot is particularly disastrous for a phalaenopsis plant because it can kill the one and only growing point. To prevent the rot, water and mist the plants in the morning so that the excess water will evaporate quickly. If you want to be absolutely certain that the plants are safe from rot, check them at nightfall on the days that you've watered them. If there is still water in the

Phalaenopsis amboinensis 'Lola Mae', HCC/AOS

Phalaenopsis violacea 'Ponkan', AM/AOS

growing point, gently soak it up with a twisted piece of tissue or paper towel.

Phalaenopsis plants are more difficult to propagate than are most other orchids because they can't be divided. However, many plants such as *Phal. lueddemanniana* and its hybrids produce keikis (see page 35) at the ends of their inflorescences. You can remove these and pot them up individually once they have a few well-developed roots. If keikis don't form on their own, you can induce them by removing the bracts from the nodes at the end of the flower stem and treating the buds with a hormone paste for keikis (available from orchid suppliers). Most of the time the paste makes the bud grow into a keiki, though sometimes it forms flowers or just a lump of callus instead. Sometimes old plants produce keikis at their bases.

Old, leggy plants can be topped to form two or more new plants. This procedure is the same as for other monopodials (see page 30–31 for instructions).

Species

Phal. amabilis This species and several of its varieties were used to breed the large white hybrid moth orchids. In fact, in the last 20 years the hybrids have become so popular that it is often difficult to find specimens of the species.

The flowers of *Phal. amabilis* are up to 3 inches across and have pure white sepals and petals. The intricate lip is yellow and white, striped and spotted with red. The clawlike antennae on the lip identify it as a member of the section Phalaenopsis. *Phal. amabilis* usually blooms from October to January. It is native to Indonesia, northern Australia, New Guinea, and the Philippines.

Phal. amboinensis One of the most striking yellow-flowered species in the Amboinensis section, this orchid has petals and sepals marked with bold reddish brown patterns. The flowers are very substantial—almost leathery—and measure about 2 inches across. They are borne in succession on spikes

that may reach 18 inches in length. Its main blooming season is spring. It grows wild on the island of Ambon, west of New Guinea.

Phal. lueddemanniana This species has confounded orchid botanists, who can't agree on whether to call it a single species with a number of different color forms or to divide it into a number of separate species. Some horticulturists, taking a conservative stance to avoid confusion in hybrid registration, continue to view *Phal. lueddemanniana* as a single species with several color forms. Herman Sweet, whose taxonomy of this genus is most widely accepted, has placed several of the forms in separate species.

Two of the most common forms placed by Herman Sweet into separate species are *Phal. hieroglyphica* and *Phal. pulchra*. The flowers of *Phal. hieroglyphica* are yellow with clusters of brown dots on the sepal and petals. *Phal. pulchra* has vivid magenta-purple flowers. One of the most common forms Sweet has

left in *Phal. lueddemanniana* is the variety *ochracea*. Its flowers are yellow with a suffusion of pale purple. If you wish to formulate your own opinion on the naming of these plants, you can find them all blooming in the spring in the Philippines.

Phal. schilleriana The leaves of this species are particularly attractive—dark green mottled with silvery gray, usually with a tinge of magenta underneath. In ideal conditions with sufficient humidity, they may reach over 12 inches long and 5 inches wide. Hundreds of the 2½-inch flowers may be carried on the long drooping sprays. The color of the sepals and petals varies somewhat, but most are white with a rosy blush. The base of the large spreading lip is spotted with red and the disk at the center is golden yellow. *Phal. schilleriana* is an old favorite and is very easy to grow. It usually blooms in spring and is found in the Philippines.

Phal. stuartiana This species is similar to *Phal. schilleriana*, but its leaves

Doritaenopsis Ravenswood 'Mister F', HCC/AOS

Phragmipedium caudatum 'El Dorado', AM/AOS

are smaller and narrower. The flowers are white and, though similar in shape to those of *Phal. schilleriana*, are tinged on the lip and lower portions of the bottom sepal with golden yellow and marked with reddish brown patches. In some plants the upper sepal and petals have patches of spots at their bases. This plant is recommended for beginners because it is easy to grow and its winter-blooming flowers last a particularly long time. Like the other moth orchids, it is native to the Philippines.

Phal. violacea This is more difficult to grow than most other *Phalaenopsis* species, but its flowers are lovely. They are borne on stout, 5-inch inflorescences. The flowers open successively over a long period; at any given time during the blooming season two or three flowers will be displayed. The top sepal and petals are mostly greenish white, but the lower half of the flower is suffused with pink to purplish rose. It flowers from spring through summer. *Phal. violacea* is native to Borneo and Malaysia.

Hybrids

The hybrids with large, rounded, white flowers now offered everywhere from florist's shops to grocery stores can all be traced back to *Phal. amabilis*. Through years of breeding, the sepals and petals have been enlarged so that they overlap to give the flower a more rounded form and have been thickened to make them sturdier and longer lasting. The overall size of the flowers has also been enlarged from the 3-inch spread found in the species to saucer-sized monsters measuring more than 5 inches across the sepals.

When it became apparent that the white forms had been "perfected," phalaenopsis breeders turned to producing colorful hybrids. Many of the pink-flowered plants now commonly available get their large rounded forms from *Phal. amabilis* and their coloration from *Phal. sanderiana* and *Phal. schilleriana*. Others result from crosses of *Phal. amabilis* with *Phal. violacea,* which, in addition to making the petals and sepals pink,

thicken the flower parts, shorten the inflorescence, and reduce the number of flowers.

Most of the latest headlines in phalaenopsis breeding concern the red-flowered hybrids. *Phal. violacea* and *Phal. amboinensis* figure in the genetic backgrounds of these striking flowers, but other species with pink or yellow flowers are used as well.

Intergeneric hybrids that include *Phalaenopsis* are also becoming quite common. One of the most important is *Doritaenopsis*, the result of *Phalaenopsis* being crossed with *Doritis pulcherrima*, which has rose-pink to deep purple flowers borne on an upright, well-branched stalk up to 3 feet tall. *Doritaenopsis* hybrids have smaller, often more deeply colored flowers than those of the phalaenopsis parent. The upright inflorescence of *Doritis* also appears in the progeny, improving the presentation of the blooms. The hybrids grow under the same easy conditions as do phalaenopsis plants.

Phragmipedium

(frag-mi-*pee*-dee-um)

Sympodial

Light   Medium to high

Temperature   Intermediate

Flowering   Spring to fall; most in spring

Care   Average

Phragmipediums are Latin American relatives of the Asian paphiopedilums. As in the paphiopedilum, the lip of a phragmipedium forms a pouch. The dorsal petal of the phragmipedium isn't as broad and brightly marked as that of a paphiopedilum, but the lateral sepals may be fantastically long. In some cases they dangle over 2½ feet. In the wild these petals may serve as ladders for pollinating insects. Several flowers are borne on each stalk.

The leathery leaves of these plants arch gracefully upward and outward from clusters at the base of the plant. They have no pseudobulbs. Phragmipediums need much brighter light than paphiopedilums, 2,400 to 3,000 footcandles, the upper end of the range required by cattleyas.

Phragmipedium schlimii 'Janet', AM/AOS

Phragmipedium Grande

Twenty-two *Phragmipedium* species have been discovered, varying from terrestrial plants that grow in the moist, well-drained loam of stream banks to true epiphytes that live in trees or on mossy rocks. Terrestrial species, such as *Phrag. longifolium*, should be potted in a mixture of sand and peat, or in sphagnum moss. Epiphytes, such as *Phrag. caudatum*, grow well in fir bark or tree fern fiber. The terrestrial plants need constant moisture (but with perfect drainage); the epiphytes are not harmed if the medium dries out slightly between waterings.

Species

Phrag. caudatum This species is commonly called the "mandarin orchid" for its supposedly oriental face and petals drooping like a mustache. Its epiphytic habit makes it more forgiving of an occasional drought than are most of the other species; for this reason it is recommended as

the best phragmipedium for windowsill culture. The flower stalk grows to about 2 feet tall and holds between 1 and 6 flowers.

The flowers of *Phrag. caudatum* are the largest of the genus. The dorsal sepal is about 6 inches long, and is pale yellow with light green veins. The petals are crimson, dangling like narrow twisted ribbons up to 3 feet below the rest of the flower. The slipper-shaped lip is yellowish white, and the most popular forms have crimson markings around the rim. *Phrag. caudatum* blooms at any time from spring to fall. It is native to a large area stretching from Mexico to Peru.

Phrag. longifolium This terrestrial species has particularly long, narrow leaves (which is how it gets the Latin name, *longifolium*), up to 32 inches long and 1½ inches wide. The flower stalk may bear more than 10 blossoms,

produced in succession over a long period. The individual flowers are waxy and long-lasting, yellow and green with rose markings. They measure about 8 inches across, but do not have extravagantly long petals. The flowering season is usually autumn, but plants sometimes bloom more than once a year. It is native to Panama, Costa Rica, and Colombia.

Hybrids

Many award-winning *Phragmipedium* hybrids have been created. Most of the hybridizing involves *Phrag. schlimii*, a terrestrial species with rounded pink and white flowers. *Phrag. caudatum* and *Phrag. longifolium* have been crossed to produce *Phrag.* Grande, a very handsome plant with green and white flowers marked with pinkish brown. As in other hybrid grexes (the term used to describe a group of seedlings; it is applied collectively to the offspring of a given cross), the flowers may vary a great deal

from plant to plant. In some cases the petals are long and dangling like those of *Phrag. caudatum;* in others they are relatively short and stiff as in *Phrag. longifolium*.

Although many breeders have tried, intergeneric hybrids of phragmipedium and paphiopedilum have not been produced with any great success. Few of these crosses produce viable seed, and those seeds that do grow generally turn into large, flowerless plants. One cross did seem to work, *Phrag.* Hanes' Magic 'Bion' (AM/AOS), the result of a cross between *Paphiopedilum stonei* 'Bion' and *Phrag.* Albopurpureum. This plant produced beautiful flowers determined by the judges to have characteristics of both parents, but scientists studying the plant's genes couldn't find any phragmipedium chromosomes. Because of this, the phragmipaphium remains but a glimmer in an orchid breeder's eye.

Sophronitis coccinea 'Edelweiss', CCM/AOS

Sophrolaelia Psyche

Sophronitis

(sof-roh-*nye*-tiss)

Sympodial

Light Medium

Temperature Intermediate

Flowering Fall to winter

Care Average to difficult

This genus name, *Sophronitis,* comes from the Greek word *sophron,* which means "modest," an appropriate description of this small genus of dwarf plants. *Sophronitis* species are best known for the scarlet-red they contribute to the flowers of hybrid cattleyas and laeliocattleyas, but their diminutive size and neat, well-formed blossoms make the plants worthwhile additions to an orchid collection.

Some taxonomists split the plants in the *Sophronitis* genus into six species; others lump them into two or three. All are native to Brazil, where they cling to moist mossy rocks and dead tree branches. Some species, such as *Soph. cernua,* grow at low elevations and thus tolerate temperatures at the warm end

of the intermediate range. *Soph. coccinea,* the most popular species, is found at higher altitudes and requires temperatures at the low end of the intermediate range for best flowering. The light requirements of sophronitis plants are similar to those of cattleyas; they adapt to a wide range of light intensities but flower best in bright light.

When it comes to water, sophronitis plants are very touchy. They must have high humidity and a moist medium. In nature the plants are often found growing in living sphagnum moss above a carpet of terrestrial bromeliads—a very moist environment indeed. Pot them in pure sphagnum or in fine fir bark with a topdressing of sphagnum. Keep the medium moist but not soggy, as with miltonia and phalaenopsis.

Sophronitis plants can be propagated by division, but they are best allowed to grow into specimen plants. The flowers are produced only by

the new growths, so large clumps with many new leads put on the most impressive display of blooms.

Species

Soph. cernua The flat, tightly clustered pseudobulbs of this species bear rigid oval leaves about 1 inch long. The bright red flowers are borne in clusters of between two and five blossoms, each about 1 inch across and almost flat when completely open. A yellow-orange patch decorates the base of the lip and column. It blooms in the winter. Native to Brazil, this species is commonly found near Rio de Janeiro.

Soph. coccinea This is by far the most important *Sophronitis* species, at least from the standpoint of cattleya breeding. The pseudobulbs and leaves are a little longer and narrower than those of *Soph. cernua,* but the plants are still only between 2 and 4 inches tall. The flowers are borne singly, and vary a great deal in size and color. Most have flowers about 1½ to

2 inches across, but in some forms the flowers may be up to 3 inches in diameter. Colors range from a rare yellow form through various shades of orange to vivid scarlet and rosy purple. The lip is usually orange with scarlet streaks. The flowers' glittery texture makes them appear iridescent. The plant produces flowers in the fall and winter from the newest mature growths. It is native to Brazil.

Hybrids

Sophronitis orchids are related to laelias and cattleyas. Breeders interested in creating red hybrid cattleyas began crossing sophronitis with species cattleyas and with hybrids of laeliocattleyas in the early days of orchid breeding. As well as adding its vivid orange or red color to cattleya and laelia hybrids, sophronitis also shifts their temperature preference toward the cool end of the intermediate range. Hybrids with *Soph. coccinea* in their backgrounds often flower two or three times a year.

Vanda coerulea 'Orchidgrove Blue Sky', HCC/AOS

Vanda sanderiana 'Triton's Treasure', HCC/AOS

Sophrolaelias combine the compact habit and vivid colors of sophronitis with the attractive flower shapes and free-blooming habit of the laelias. A popular old hybrid, *Sophrolaelia* Psyche *(Laelia cinnabarina × Sophronitis coccinea)*, has yielded several prize-winning selections including 'China', which was recently awarded an AM/AOS. Its clusters of bright orange flowers may appear two or three times a year. These plants thrive under fluorescent lights.

Sophrolaeliocattleyas (commonly abbreviated *Slc.*) are widely grown hybrids involving laelias, sophronitises, and cattleyas. The flowers of these miniature and semi-miniature plants run the gamut from clear yellow to sparkling red, with many blushes and hues in between. *Sophrolaeliocattleya* Hazel Boyd and *Slc.* Jewel Box are two of the most popular hybrids, but hundreds of others are available. Numerous high-quality awarded cultivars are offered by nurseries.

Vanda

*(van-*dah)

Monopodial

Light High

Temperature Intermediate to warm

Flowering Any season; most species spring to summer

Care Average

Vandas are some of the most popular cultivated orchids. The broad spectrum of their flower colors includes purple, brown, yellow, white, red, and blue—colors that have been mixed in fantastic combinations and patterns by hybridizers. The flowers are large and long-lived, and often appear more than once a year. They are produced from the points where the leaves join the stem.

Vanda plants have an interesting shape; the thick upright stems bear opposite ranks of leaves nourished by a tangle of aerial roots. As with the other monopodial orchids, all new growth takes place at the top of the plant. Some species grow very tall—up to 6 feet—but you can keep them

at a manageable size by topping them when they get too tall. Most of the hybrids have fairly compact growth habits.

Vanda species are divided into two types, distinguished by the shape of the leaves. Most of the species have straplike leaves, folded into a V near the point where the leaf joins the stem. The other group has cylindrical leaves called terete leaves. Hybridizers have created a third group with semiterete leaves by crossing strap-leaved species with terete-leaved species.

Vandas with terete or semiterete leaves need intense sunlight and only flower well outdoors in full sun. The strap-leaved types, however, perform well on bright windowsills and in greenhouses or lath houses.

Both pots and baskets work well for vandas. Coarse bark and tree fern fiber are the most widely used growing mediums. The fast-growing plants don't like to be crowded, so expect to repot them frequently when they are young. When the plants reach flowering size, repot

them only to replace the growing medium when it decays. The plants need abundant water and plenty of fertilizer during the growing season, and should not be allowed to dry out completely between waterings. When you water the growing medium, water the aerial roots as well. To avoid splashing water, use a mist bottle to moisten the aerial roots.

Species

Vanda coerulea This famous blue-flowered species is widely grown and extensively hybridized. The symmetrical, rounded petals and sepals are pale blue, netted with veins of deeper blue. The flower sprays are dramatic; 5 to 15 of the flowers are held in each spray, and individual flowers may be up to 4 inches across. The plants grow up to 4 feet tall, but are easily kept below 2 feet. The strap-shaped leaves are about 10 inches long and 1 inch wide. Many fine cultivars are available,

Ascocenda Buddy Choo 'Solo's Ed', HCC/AOS

with flower colors ranging from pale to midnight blue. Native to the highlands of Thailand, Burma, and India, *V. coerulea* needs cool night temperatures. It flowers in the fall and winter.

Euanthe sanderiana (V. sanderiana) Although botanists placed this species in a new genus *Euanthe* because of its unique lip, most horticultural books and catalogs still list this species with the other vandas. Whatever you choose to call it, this is one of the most magnificent of all orchids, producing fragrant, well-shaped flowers from 3½ to 4½ inches across. The petals and sepals are broad and rounded, and open flat. The color is an exquisite combination of white, yellow, crimson, and brown. The species has many variously colored forms, ranging in overall hue from purple to red. Four to ten of the flowers are borne on each inflorescence. The leaves are strap-shaped, and are usually

about 15 inches long. Native to the Philippines, *E. sanderiana* prefers intermediate to warm conditions. It blooms in the fall.

Hybrids
Because flowers are the focus of hybridization, the flowers of hybrid vandas are generally superior to those of the species. In many cases the hybrids are also more vigorous than the species are. Undoubtedly the most famous hybrid is *V.* Rothschildiana, a cross of *V. coerulea* and *E. sanderiana.* This hybrid flowers as freely as *V. coerulea,* and this parent also gives the flowers their touch of blue and the netted pattern on the sepals and petals. From *V. sanderiana* come a particularly attractive flower shape and an intriguing lip structure. *Vanda* Rothschildiana requires temperatures in the intermediate range.

Vanda species have also been crossed with species in a number of other genera. Some of these intergeneric hybrids

are better than the pure vanda hybrids for home growing because they require less space and can get by on less light. Smaller hybrids made with *Vanda* and *Ascocentrum* species, known as ascocendas, are especially well-suited to light gardens and other spots where space is limited. Breeders in Hawaii and Thailand have been working on ascocendas and related hybrids for years; it is possible now to find flowers in all the vanda colors as well as tones not found in pure vandas. The flowers of ascocendas are smaller than those of vandas—about the size of a quarter—but they make up in bright color and fine form what they may lack in size. Another fine small hybrid genus suitable for windowsill and light gardens is *Rhynchovanda (Vanda* × *Rhynchostylis).* Seedlings and mericlones of intergeneric *Vanda* hybrids are widely available.

Glossary
The world of orchids is filled with technical words. Following are definitions of the terms used in this book.

AM Award of Merit. Awarded to plants receiving 80 to 89 points in formal judging.

AOS American Orchid Society.

Aerial roots Roots produced above or out of the growing medium.

Agar A gelatinous substance derived from certain seaweeds and used to solidify culture mediums. Culture mediums are used for germinating orchid seed and for propagating plants through meristem culture.

Albino A plant with a marked deficiency in pigmentation, such as a white-flowered form of a usually colorful species.

Apical At or pertaining to the tip of any structure. Usually used to refer to the tip of a stem.

Axil The angle between a branch or leaf and the stem (or axis) from which it arises.

Backbulb An old pseudobulb, often without leaves but still alive and bearing one or more buds. Located behind the actively growing portion of a sympodial orchid.

Basal Of, at, or forming at the base.

Bicolor Two-colored.

Bifoliate Two-leaved. Commonly used to refer to the number of leaves arising from a pseudobulb.

Botanical A term designating any species or genus of orchid that is not grown commercially for its flowers.

Callus A hard protuberance or thickening on a flower part.

Capsule The seed pod.

Chlorotic Abnormally yellowed, due to a breakdown of the chlorophyll.

Clone An individual plant raised from a single seed, and all its subsequent vegetative propagations.

Column The central organ of an orchid flower, formed by the male and female parts.

Community pot A pot containing numerous small orchid seedlings or clones, transplanted from a flask.

Crest A toothed, fringed, or hairy thickened portion on the disk of the lip on an orchid flower.

Cross-pollinate To transfer the pollen from a flower on one plant to the stigma of a flower on another plant.

Cultivar An individual plant and its vegetative propagations in cultivation; a cultivated variety.

Deciduous A plant that sheds its leaves at maturity, or at the end of the growing season.

Division The technique of propagating plants by cutting or breaking apart the pseudobulbs or stems at the rhizome; a single propagation produced in that manner.

Dorsal Of or pertaining to the back, as of an organ or part, such as the uppermost sepal of an orchid flower.

Equitant Conduplicate (folded lengthwise) leaves that overlap one another in two ranks, as in *Oncidium*.

Epiphyte A plant that naturally grows upon another plant or other object above the soil. Epiphytic plants are not parasitic; they derive their nourishment from the organic matter that accumulates around their roots and photosynthesize their own carbohydrates.

Evergreen Retaining green foliage all year, as certain species of *Dendrobium*, in contrast to deciduous species.

Eye The incipient bud of a vegetative growth, particularly in sympodial orchids.

FCC First Class Certificate. Awarded to plants receiving 90 points or more in formal judging.

Flat Shallow tray or box in which numerous very small seedlings are grown.

Genera Plural of genus.

Genus A subdivision of a family consisting of one or more species that show similar characteristics and appear to have common ancestry.

Grex A group of seedlings; applied collectively to the offspring of a given cross.

HCC Highly Commended Certificate. Awarded to plants receiving 75 to 79 points in formal judging.

Habit The characteristic form of a plant.

Hapuu Hawaiian word for tree fern fiber.

Humus Decomposing organic matter on or in the soil.

Intergeneric Between or among two or more genera.

Internode That portion of a stem between two nodes.

Interspecific Between or among two or more species.

Introduced Brought from another region, intentionally or otherwise. In horticulture, refers to the intentional bringing of plants into cultivation either from another country or from the wild.

Keiki A Hawaiian term referring to an offshoot or offset from a plant.

Labellum The modified petal of an orchid flower. Commonly called the lip.

Lead A new vegetative growth on a plant.

Lip The labellum, a modified petal in an orchid flower, usually differing markedly in size, coloration, and form from the other two petals.

Lithophyte A plant that naturally grows on rocks. It derives its nutrients from the organic matter that accumulates around its roots.

Mask The colored spot on the base of the lip in miltonias.

Microchilum Small-lipped.

Monopodial A form of growth in which there is a single vegetative shoot that continues to grow from its terminal bud from season to season, such as in the genus *Vanda*.

Mutation A sudden departure from the parent type, due to a change in a chromosome or gene; an individual resulting from such a departure.

Natural hybrid A hybrid produced in the wild.

Nocturnal Of the night; used in reference to flowers that open after dark.

Node A joint on a stem or pseudobulb that normally bears a leaf, bract, or a whorl of leaves.

Nomenclature A set of names or system of naming.

Overwater Keeping the growing medium overly moist by watering too frequently. This can destroy the roots and predispose a plant to infection by fungi and bacteria.

Pistil The female, seed-producing organ of the flower, consisting of the ovary, stigma, and style (when present).

Pseudobulb A thickened portion of a stem resembling a bulb. Common among epiphytic orchids.

Rhizome A root-bearing stem, prostrate on or under the surface, the apex of which progressively sends up leafy shoots.

Rostellum A little beak; a slender extension from the upper edge of the stigma.

SLC The abbreviation for *Sophrolaeliocattleya*.

Selection A breeding process involving the crossing of parents that have outstanding characteristics in order to produce improved offspring.

Semi-alba A white flower that has a colored lip.

Sepal One of the outer three parts of an orchid flower.

Shell-type A group of *Encyclia* species in which the upright labellum resembles a shell.

Specimen An individual exemplifying a group; a large, well-cultivated plant.

Sphagnum A bog moss of the genus *Sphagnum*, used dried or alive in some kinds of potting media to retain moisture.

Stamen The male organ of the flower, which bears the pollen.

Stigma The part of the pistil that is receptive to pollen.

Substance The firmness and durability of a flower.

Succulent Soft and juicy; fleshy; adapted to the retention of water.

Synonym A scientific name rejected in favor of a more correct name for a species.

Taxonomy The science of classification, concerned with the arrangement of plants (or animals) into groups according to natural relationships.

Terete Cylindrical; circular in cross section.

Terrestrial Growing on the ground and supported by soil or the layer of humus on the surface of the soil.

Tree fern A large tropical or subtropical fern, generally of the family *Cyatheaceae*, which has a fibrous trunk used as a potting medium for orchids. It can be used in shredded form in containers, or as logs, slabs, or blocks. Also known by the Hawaiian term *hapuu*.

Tribe A group of related genera.

Trigeneric Of or pertaining to three genera, usually in reference to hybrids derived from the combination of parents in three genera.

Unifoliate Having one leaf per pseudobulb.

INDEX

Note: Boldface type indicates reference to principal discussion. Italic type indicates illustrations.

A

Air, movement of. *See* Ventilation
Aliceara, 69, 80
  Hawaiian Delight 'Sunshine', 80
AM/AOS. *See* Award of Merit
American Orchid Society Bulletin, 50, 56, 61
Angraecum sesquipedale, 7
AOS. *See* Society, American Orchid
Ascocenda, 92
Ascocentrum, 92
Award of Merit (AM/AOS), 67
Awards, 67
Awards Quarterly, 56, 61

B

Ballast, for fluorescent light, 47
Bargains, in orchids, 60
Bark, for potting, 24
  fir, 25, 29
  redwood, 28
Barton, Barbara, 61
Bench, for greenhouse, 51
Books, on orchids, 61
Botrytis cinerea (petal blight), 42, *43*
Brassavola, 15, 18, **68–69**
  cucullata, 68
  David Sander, 68, *68*
  digbyana. See Rhyncholaelia digbyana
  hybrids, 68
  nodosa, 68
Brassia, 15, 18, 64, 66, **68–69**
  Edvah Loo, 69
    'Mark Daniel', *69*
  gireoudiana, *54*, 68–69
    'Town Hill', *69*
  hybrids, 69
  longissima, 69
  maculata, 69
    'Monte Vista', *69*
  verrucosa, 69
Brassidium, 80
  Florida Gem 'Sylvia', 80
  Zanzibar Princess 'Anne', *69*
Brassocattleya, 68
Brassolaelia, 75
Brassolaeliocattleya, 68, 70, 75
  Clyde's Melody 'Orchidglade', *71*
Bulbophyllum falcatum, 49

C

Cable, for heating, 20
Camera, using, to measure light, 14
Catalog, deciphering mail-order, 58
Cattleya, 15, 18, 49, *62*, 66, **69–71**

Cattleya (continued)
  aurantiaca, 70
  'Sally', *69*
  bicolor, 70
    'Orchidglade', *70*
  blooming, in captivity, 5
  guttata, 70
  hybrids, 70–71
  labiata, 49, 63, 69, 70
  mossiae, 49
  percivaliana, 49
  skinneri, 70
    'Many', *70*
  trianae, 49
CBR/AOS. *See* Certificate, of Botanical Recognition
CCM/AOS. *See* Certificate, of Cultural Merit
Cercospora (leaf spot fungus), 42, *42*
Certificate
  of Botanical Recognition (CBR/AOS), 67
  of Cultural Merit (CCM/AOS), 67
  First Class (FCC/AOS), 67
  Highly Commended (HCC/AOS), 67
  of Horticultural Merit (CHM/AOS), 67, *67*
Charcoal, for potting, 28
CHM/AOS. *See* Certificate, of Horticultural Merit
Clay, expanded, for potting, 26
Cloning, meristem, 36–37
Cochlioda, 49
Colletotrichum (leaf spot fungus), 42, *42*
Colmanara, 80
Conditions, modifying, to grow orchids, 13
Containers, 25
Cooling, for greenhouse, 52
Cork
  for potting, 27
  slabs of, 34
Coryanthes speciosa, 8
Cost, of artificial lighting, 46
Cryptanthemis slateri, 10
Culture
  problems of improper (chart), 38–40
  under lights, 48–49
  orchids suitable for, 49
Cymbidium, 15, 18, *53*, **71**
  Bulbarrow 'Pinkie', *71*
  hybrids, 71
  miniature, *62*, 71
Cypripedium calceolus
  var. *parviflorum* 'Carrie Ann', *9*

D

Darwin, Charles, 7
Day length, adjusting, 48–49
Dendrobium, 15, 18, 49, **72–73**
  affine, 73
  aggregatum, 72
    'M.G.R.', *72*
  Anna Bibus, 73
  anosmum, 72

Dendrobium (continued)
  antennatum, 72
  atroviolaceum, 73
  bellatulum, 73
  bigibbum, 73
  canaliculatum, 72
  chrysanthum, 72
  chrysotoxum, 72
    'Fred Fuchs, Jr.', *72*
  crassinode, 72
  cuthbertsonii, 49
  dearii, 73
  densiflorum, 72
  dicuphum, 73
  discolor, 72
  draconis, 73
  falconeri, 72
  farmeri, 72
  fimbriatum, 72
  findleyanum, 72
  formosum, 73
  friedricksianum, 72
  gouldii, 72
  Hagaromo 'Spring Fuji', 73
  heterocarpum, 72
  Hickam Deb, 73
  hybrids, 73
    Yamamoto cross, 73
  infundibulum, 73
  johannis, 72
  johnsoniae, 73
    'Mission Bay', *73*
  kingianum, 49
  Lady Hamilton, 73
  lineale, 72
  loddigesii, 72
  lowii, 73
  lyonii, 73
  macrophyllum, 73
  margaritaceum, 73
  Marianne Bates, 73
  moniliforme, 72
  Orglade's Orbit, 73
  parishii, 72
  phalaenopsis, 49, 73
    'Dawn', *73*
  primulinum, 72
  Ram Misra, 73
  sanderae, 73
  São Paulo 'Memory', 73
  schuetzii, 73
  sections, 72–73
    Callista, 72
    Dendrobium, 72
    Formosae, 73
    Latouria, 73
    Phalaenanthe, 73
    Spatulata, 72
  spectabile, 73
  stratiotes, 72
  strebloceras, 72
  taurinum, 72
  thyrsiflorum, 72
  transparens, 72
  treating, to promote flowering, 24
  Utopia 'Messenger', 73
  wardianum, 72
  williamsonianium, 73
  Yukidaruma 'King', 73

Disease, problems caused by, **42–43**
  blight, 42, *43*
  fungus, 42, *42*, *43*
  spot, 42, *43*
  virus, 43, *43*, 61
Dividing plants, procedure for, 30, 35
Doritaenopsis, 88
  Ravenswood 'Mister F', *88*
Doritis pulcherrima, 88

E

Encyclia
  See also Epidendrum
  adenocaula, 74
  cochleata, 49, 74
  cordigera, *73*, 74
  fragrans, 74
  hybrids, 74
  tampensis, 49, 74, *74*
Epicattleya, 71
  Honey 'Gene Dangler', *74*
Epidendrum, 15, 18, **73–74**
  See also Encyclia
  atropurpureum, 74
  ciliare, 74
  cochleatum, 74
  fragrans, 74
  hybrids, 74
  tampense, 74
Equipment
  for greenhouses, 51–53, 61
  sources for, 61
Euanthe sanderiana, 92

F

FCC/AOS. *See* Certificate, First Class
Fertilizer, **23–24**
  applying, 24
  nutrient content of, 23–24
  and potting medium, 26–28
  tips for using, 24
  types of, 23–24
Fertilizing, problems of, 38
Fiber, for potting
  osmunda, 28
  tree fern, 24, 26, 28, 29
Fixture, for fluorescent light, 46
Flasks, seedlings in, 37
Flower
  durability of, 9
  structure of, 8–9
Flowering, to promote, 24, 25
  darkness required for, 49
Footcandle, as a measurement of light, 14
Fusarium oxysporum cattleya (root rot fungus), 42, *42*

G

Gardening by Mail (Barton), 61
Glossary, 92–93
Gravel
  for humidity trays, 19–20
  for potting, 26

Greenhouse, *44,* **49–53**
  attached, 49–50
  building, 50–51
  equipment for, 51–53, 61
  freestanding, 50
  prefabricated, sources
    for, 61
  situating, 50
  stove house as, 6
Growth, pattern of, 10–11

H
Habitat, 9–10
Haemaria discolor. See
  Ludisia discolor
Handbook on Orchid
  Culture, 56
HCC/AOS. *See* Certificate,
  Highly Commended
Heating
  for greenhouse, 51
  and humidity, 20–21
Home Orchid Growing
  (Northen), 37, 61
Houseplants, orchids as, **13–43**
How to Build & Use
  Greenhouses (Ortho),
  51, 61
Humidifier
  greenhouse, 52–53
  to use, 21
Humidity, **19–21**
  tips for improving, 20
  to measure, 19
  to raise, 19–29
Hybrids
  intergeneric, 66
  naming of, 65
  prices for, 6
Hygrometer, *19*

K, L
Keikis (offshoots), 35–36, 73, 87
Laelia, 15, 18, 49, 66, **75**
  anceps, 75
  cinnabarina, 91
  hybrids, 75
  Psyche 'China', 91
  pumila, 75
    'Sanbar Classic', *75*
  purpurata, 75
  'Velvet Dusk', *75*
Laeliocattleya, 49, 71, 75
Lamp
  high-power sodium, 46
  mercury vapor, 46
  quartz, 46
Lava rock, for potting, 26
Light
  artificial, 45, **46–49**
  sources for, 61
  fluorescent, 45–46
  intensity of, to maximize, 48
  to measure, 14–15
  meter, 14, *15*
  to modify, 16
  problems with, 38, 40
  requirements, **14–17,** 15
    (chart), 16, 46
  species sensitive to, 49
  tips for using, 16

Light garden, 45, *46*
Lindleyana, 56, 61
Ludisia, 15, 18, **76**
  discolor (Haemaria
    discolor), 49, 76
  'Smitchen', *76*
  var. *dawsoniana, 76*

M
Macodes petola, 49
Mail order, 57–60
  addresses for, 61
Maintenance, of artificial
  lights, 49
Masdevallia, 15, 18, 49, **76–77**
  Angel Frost, 77
  coccinea, 76
  floribunda, 77
  hybrids, 7
  infracta, 77
    'Devine', *77*
  Marguerite, 77
  peristeria, 77
  strobelii, 77
  tovarensis, 77
  veitchiana, 76, 77
    'Mem. Mary Chantry', *76*
Mask, described, 79
Mericloning (meristemming).
  See Cloning, meristem
Miltassia, 65, 69
  Aztec 'Purple Star', *80*
  Charles M. Fitch, 49
  'Dark Monarch', 49
Miltonia, 15, 18, 49, 64–66,
  77–79
  'Anne Warne', 79
  × Bluntii, 64, 79, *79*
  Celle, 79
  clowesii, 64, 79
    'Warren Street', *77,* 78
  hybrids, 79
    intergeneric, 79
  regnellii, 78
  spectabilis, 64, 66, 78
    var. *moreliana,* 64, 78, 79
    'Elizabeth Grenis', *78*
  vexillaria, 78–79
    'Giselle', *78*
Miltonidium, 80
Miltoniopsis, 78
  vexillaria, 78–79
Minerals, excess, to eliminate, 24
Mirrors, to augment light, *46*
Misting, 21
Monopodial
  dividing, 30
  growth pattern of, 10, 11
  to plant, 32
  pot size for, 31
Moss, for potting
  peat, 27
  sphagnum, 27

N
Names
  common, 66
  conventions of, for orchids,
  64–66
Nature Conservancy, The, 59

Northen, Rebecca, 37, 61
Nurseries, for orchids, 57, *60*

O
Odontioda, 80
Odontobrassia, 80
  Inca 'Royal Indian', *80*
Odontocidium, 80
Odontoglossum, 15, 18, 49, 64,
  66, **79–80**
  crispum, 79
  grande, 78, 80
  hybrids, 80
  luteo-purpureum, 79
  odoratum, 79
  pulchellum, 80
Odontonia, 80
Offshoots. *See* Keikis
Oncidium, 8, *11,* 15, 18, 49, 64,
  81–83
  ampliatum, 81
  carthagenense, 81
  cheirophorum, 81
  crispum, 81–82
    'J & L', *81*
  hybrids, 83
  luridum, 82
  macranthum, 82
  papilio, 82
    'Robert Parke', *82*
  sphacelatum, 82
  splendidum, 49, 81, 82
    'Robert', *81*
  tigrinum, 82, *82*
  triquetrum, 81, 82
  varicosum, 83
  var. *rogersii,* 83
Ophrys, 7
Orchid
  species
    awards for, 67
    numbers of, 9
  varieties
    awards for, 67
    naming of, 64–65
Orchid Advocate, The, 56, 61
Orchidelirium, 5
Orchids
  choosing, 57
  endangered, 59
  epiphytic, 10, 22
  obtaining, 56–61
  potted, caring for, 60
  subterranean, 10
  terrestrial, 10
Outdoors, growing orchids, 53

P
Paphiopedilum, 15, 18, 49,
  83–85
  bellatulum, 84
    'Vasco', *83*
  callosum, 84, 85
    'Jac', 85
    'Rayber', *83*
    'Sparkling Burgundy', 85
  chamberlanianum
    'Magnifico', *67*
  coloratum, 85
  Delrosi, 4, back cover

Paphiopedilum (continued)
  to divide, 30
  Faire-Maude, 85
  fairieanum, 84–85
    'Maj', *84*
  green-leaved, 84–85
  hybrids, *57,* 85
  insigne, 85
  Kay Rinaman 'Val', *4*
  lawrenceanum, 85
  Makuli, 85
  Maudiae, 85
    'Diamond Jubilee', 85
    'Dorothy Ann', 85, *85*
    'Los Osos', *4,* 85
    'Pinot Noir', *85*
    'St. Francis', 85
  mottled-leaved, 84
  Neptune 'Mars', *4*
  philippinense, 85
  Sioux 'Teal', 85, *85*
  stonei 'Bion', 89
  sukhakulii, 84, 85
  venustum, 84
    'McQuerry', *84*
  vinicolorum, 85
  Winston Churchill
    'Indomitable', *4*
Periodicals, on orchids, 61
Perlite, 25
  for potting, 27
Pests, problems caused by,
  40–41
  aphids, 40
  mealybugs, 40
  scales, 41
  snails and slugs, 40
  spider mites, 40
  virus, 41
Phalaenopsis, 11, 12, 15, 18, 36,
  49, **86–88**
  amabilis, 49, 86, 87, 88
    'Truford', *86*
  amboinensis, 87, 88
    'Lola Mae', *87*
  hieroglyphica, 87
  hybrids, 88
  keikis of, 36
  lueddemanniana, 87
    'Jo-San', *86*
  var. *ochracea,* 87
  pulchra, 87
  sanderiana, 88
  schilleriana, 86, 87, 88
    'Classic', *86*
  stuartiana, 86, 87–88
  violacea, 88
    'Ponkan', *87*
Phragmipedium, 15, 18, 49,
  88–89
  Albopurpureum, 89
  caudatum, 89
    'El Dorado', *89*
  Grande, 89, *89*
  Hanes' Magic 'Bion', 89
  hybrids, 89
  longifolium, 89
  schlimii, 89
    'Janet', *89*
Phytophthora cactorum (black
  rot fungus), 42, *43*

Pollination, 7–8, 9
Pollinia, 7–8, 9
Pot
    removing orchids from,
        29–30
    size of, 30–31
Potinara, 71
Potting. *See* Repotting
Potting medium, **25–28**
    fertilizer and, 24, 26
    man-made, 26
Problems, diagnosis of, **37–43**
Propagation, **35–39**
Pseudobulb, 10
    planting dormant, 35
    removing sheath of, 37
Pseudomonas cattleyae
    (bacterial brown spot),
        42, *43*
Pythium ultimatum (black rot
    fungus), 42, *43*

R
Repotting, **29–34**
    procedure for, 29–32
    and subsequent care, 32
    timing, 29
    tips for, 32
Rhizanthella gardneri, 10
Rhizoctonia solani (root rot
    fungus), 42, *42*
Rhizome, 11
    to divide, 30
RHS. *See* Society, Royal
    Horticultural

Rhynchostylis, 92
Rhynchovanda, 92
Rhyncholaelia digbyana, 68
    'Dragonstone', *68*
Root
    aerial, 22
    bare, caring for, 60
    to clean, 30
Rossioglossum, 79
    grande, 80

S
*Sander's Complete List of
    Orchid Hybrids* (RHS), 65
Scent, as attractant, 8
Seed, *7,* 35
Shale, expanded, for potting, 26
Societies, orchid, 56
    addresses of, 61
    as a source of plants, 60
Society
    American Orchid (AOS),
        48, 56
    awards of, 67
    Cymbidium, of America, 56
    Royal Horticultural (RHS), 65
Soil, leaching minerals out of,
    23, 24
Sophrolaelia, 91
    Psyche, *90*
Sophrolaeliocattleya, 66, 71, 91
    Hazel Boyd, 91
    Jewel Box, 91

Sophronitis, 15, 18, 49, 65,
    90–91
    cernua, 90
    coccinea, 90, 91
    'Edelweiss', *90*
    hybrids, 90
Sterilization, of tools, 29, 37
Stress, in orchids, 37
Summer, orchids outdoors
    during, 53
Support, providing, 32
Sweet, Herman, 87
Sympodial
    dividing, 30
    growth pattern of, 10–11
    pot size for, 30–31
    to plant, 31–32

T
Temperature, **17–19**
    categories of, 17
    daily fluctuation of, 17
    to measure, 17
    requirements, 17, 18
        (chart), 19
    tips for regulating, 19
Testing service, for virus
    infections, 41, 61
Thermometer, maximum-
    minimum, *17*
Transplanting, 34

Tray, gravel-filled, for humidity,
    19–29
Tree fern
    fiber. *See* Fiber
    slabs of, for orchids, 34

V
Vanda, 15, 18, **91–92**
    coerulea, 91–92
        'Orchidgrove Blue Sky', *91*
    hybrids, 92
    Rothschildiana, 92
    *sanderiana (Euanthe
        sanderiana),* 92
        'Triton's Treasure', *91*
Velamen, 22
Ventilation, **21–22**
    for greenhouse, 52
    problems with, 38
Vuylsteke, C., 66
Vuylstekeara, 80
    Cambria 'Plush', 80, *80*
    Edna 'Stamperland', *80*

W, X, Y, Z
Watering, **22–23**
    problems of, 38
    procedure for, 23
    timing, 22–23
    tips for, 23
Wilsonara, 80
Wood, slabs of, for orchids, 34
World Wildlife Fund, 59
Zoufaly, Howard, 48

U.S. Measure and Metric Measure Conversion Chart

		Formulas for Exact Measures			Rounded Measures for Quick Reference		
	Symbol	When you know:	Multiply by:	To find:			
Mass	oz	ounces	28.35	grams	1 oz		= 30 g
(Weight)	lb	pounds	0.45	kilograms	4 oz		= 115 g
	g	grams	0.035	ounces	8 oz		= 225 g
	kg	kilograms	2.2	pounds	16 oz	= 1 lb	= 450 g
					32 oz	= 2 lb	= 900 g
					36 oz	= 2¼ lb	= 1000g (1 kg)
Volume	pt	pints	0.47	liters	1 c	= 8 oz	= 250 ml
	qt	quarts	0.95	liters	2 c (1 pt)	= 16 oz	= 500 ml
	gal	gallons	3.785	liters	4 c (1 qt)	= 32 oz	= 1 liter
	ml	milliliters	0.034	fluid ounces	4 qt (1 gal)	= 128 oz	= 3¾ liter
Length	in.	inches	2.54	centimeters	⅜ in.	= 1 cm	
	ft	feet	30.48	centimeters	1 in.	= 2.5 cm	
	yd	yards	0.9144	meters	2 in.	= 5 cm	
	mi	miles	1.609	kilometers	2½ in.	= 6.5 cm	
	km	kilometers	0.621	miles	12 in. (1 ft)	= 30 cm	
	m	meters	1.094	yards	1 yd	= 90 cm	
	cm	centimeters	0.39	inches	100 ft	= 30 m	
					1 mi	= 1.6 km	
Temperature	°F	Fahrenheit	⅝ (after subtracting 32)	Celsius	32°F	= 0°C	
	°C	Celsius	⅝ (then add 32)	Fahrenheit	212°F	= 100°C	
Area	in.²	square inches	6.452	square centimeters	1 in.²	= 6.5 cm²	
	ft²	square feet	929.0	square centimeters	1 ft²	= 930 cm²	
	yd²	square yards	8361.0	square centimeters	1 yd²	= 8360 cm²	
	a.	acres	0.4047	hectares	1 a.	= 4050 m²	